AC

ACT YOUR AGE

Frank Topping

HODDER AND STOUGHTON
LONDON SYDNEY AUCKLAND TORONTO

Licence to perform the sketches in this volume

The copyright to all sketches resides with the author, Frank Topping. Permission from the copyright holder must be sought before any of the works are performed. Such permission will be granted for specific performances, after written application has been received.

However, for performances where *no* money will change hands (i.e. no tickets will be sold), such permission will be automatically granted free of charge and requests are therefore not necessary.

Requests for all paying performances (whether for charitable purposes or not) must be made to:

The Rev. Frank Topping
c/o Hodder and Stoughton Limited
47 Bedford Square
London WC1B 3DP

British Library Cataloguing in Publication Data

Topping, Frank, *1937–*
Act your age
I. Title
822'.914

ISBN 0-340-50212-6

Published by Hodder and Stoughton Limited, Mill Road, Dunton Green, Sevenoaks, Kent TN13 2YE. Editorial Office: 47 Bedford Square, London WC1B 3DP. Photoset by Rowland Phototypesetting Limited, Bury St Edmunds, Suffolk. Printed in Great Britain by Richard Clay Limited, Bungay, Suffolk.

Contents

Introduction

In 1869 the 'New Cut', off the Waterloo Road in London where the 'Old Vic' now stands, was notorious for crime, poverty and vice. 'Thieves' Kitchens', described so vividly by Charles Dickens, flourished. In the surrounding back alleys of Lambeth homeless children slept rough, in any way or place they could. They could be found sleeping in empty packing cases, tubs and barrels, or across gratings from which warm air escaped.

This area was the cradle of the National Children's Home. On the 9th July 1869, in a rented two roomed cottage and stable in a small street off the Waterloo Road, the National Children's Home was born. On that day the first two children were received into the home.

The founder of that home, who was to devote the rest of his life to the care of children in need, was the local Wesleyan Methodist minister, The Rev. Dr. Thomas Bowman Stephenson. His work was to become a pioneering light in the darkness of poverty, neglect and need. Today that light burns as brightly as ever in the continuing work of the NCH. As society changes, so do the dangers which threaten children, and the NCH has had to change too. It is a tribute to those committed to this work that the NCH is still in the vanguard, still pioneering in the work of child care.

1989 is a very special year for NCH: it is the 150th anniversary of the birth of Dr. Stephenson, the 120th anniversary of the NCH, and the 80th birthday of its Chairman, George Thomas, Lord Tonypandy. This book is a tribute to the NCH past and present, a small contribution to the celebration of some very special birthdays.

Happy birthday George, Happy birthday NCH, and many happy returns.

Frank Topping, Kent, 1988

Foreword by John Craven

I've known Frank Topping for many years – he is a remarkable man with a burning faith. To combine the gifts of writer, comic, entertainer, theologian and practising minister is formidable. To use them all at once and, in so doing, turn the whole approach to things religious or moral on its head, is amazing.

This delightful book continues the Topping style that we know well from his radio and television performances. Who else would re-write the nativity story and make it happen on the Liverpool ferry, who else would take the heavenly host of angels and turn them into a military squad, supporting fallen mankind? In *Act Your Age*, these and many other playlets and poems are written for performance, at any level but mainly for the School or Church group who wish to get a serious message across in an amusing way. But the book can also be a good read for anyone who wants to look beneath the crusty surface of dry religion.

About three years ago, I was asked to report on the work of NCH in a film called *NCH Newsdesk*. I went from a Rochdale Family Centre to a Leeds phone-in service, to a Salford centre for young offenders, to a West country unit for disabled children, to a multi-racial community project in South London, and to me it was a revelation. I had not realised just how much still needs to be done to help Britain's disadvantaged young people, and how much NCH is, in fact, doing. Some of the stories I heard – from young mothers on the verge of suicide, from teenagers desperately trying to get out of a life of crime, from NCH workers battling on despite huge problems – will stay with me forever.

I became an NCH Supporter and found, to my delight, that two very special friends of NCH were George

Thomas and Frank Topping. It was a great joy, therefore, that in this book all three came together. For 1989 is NCH Birthday Year and one of the major birthday celebrations surrounds George who is 80 this year and for five years, Chairman of NCH. And Frank, in a characteristic ouburst of generosity, has compiled this collection as his own inimitable celebration of NCH Birthday Year.

And celebrate we shall.

John Craven

Whose Children?

To whom do they belong
these children;
when Christopher Robin kneels to pray
and little Miss Muffet runs away,
and children clap their hands for joy:

when sunlight bounces
on silken hair
and hop-scotch skipping
fills the air
with shouts and laughter;

and tragic girls
knuckle hot, wet cheeks
and grubby boys
grieve broken toys
or comforters, lost?

To whom do they belong,
these children?
Neat or tattered
healthy or battered
what have they to do with us?

Do we suffer
their innocence,
pleased in them to see
the Christ-patterned key
to Paradise?

Or are they weaned
on broken promises;

cheated by deceit
and oh so bitter-sweet
hopes and dreams;

where infant pain
licks its wounds
and love-starved trust
eats the dust
of empty words?

And is God silent,
aloof, unmoved?
Or, beyond relief,
does His grief
sound depths too deep
for mortal hearing?

And does He weep for all,
weep timelessly;
weep for children in danger
weep, in that rough manger,
where love's child was born?

To whom do they belong,
these children,
loved, adored,
hurt, ignored,
what have they to do
with us?

Mums and Dads

(Because there is an underlying sense of pathos in this scene it is best played by adult actors, unless exceptionally talented child actors are available.)

PETER *is neat and clean,* JASON *is a bit of a mess. Both boys are dressed in shirts, short grey flannels, school ties and stockings.*

Music: Non-vocal version of 'Girls and Boys Come Out to Play'.

Curtain and/or lights up on PETER *and* JASON *struggling for possession of a tennis ball.*

JASON: It's mine! My Dad give it me! It's from Japan!
PETER: *(Frustrated, begins an old game.)* Well, well my Dad's bigger than your Dad!
JASON: No he isn't, my Dad's so big he has to bend down to go through doors!
PETER: That's 'cos you live in a teeny-weeny house! *(Pause)* Anyway, my Dad, my Dad's a boxer, and he'll thump your Dad!
JASON: My Dad's a wrestler, an' an' an' he'll throw your Dad on his back!
PETER: Yeah? Well, my Dad, my Dad's got a car, a *red* one, and it goes a hundred miles an hour!
JASON: *(A bit defeated, sniffs.)* I know, I've seen it. *(Pause)* Well, it's still my ball and you're not playing! Anyway, your Dad's not a boxer, 'cos I've seen him, and he hasn't got a broken nose!
PETER: That's 'cos nobody could hit him on his nose!

And your Dad's not a wrestler, 'cos he's got grey hair and a fing in his ear 'cos he's deaf!

JASON: No he hasn't!

PETER: Yes he has!

JASON: He 'asn't!

PETER: He 'as!

JASON: 'As'nt!

PETER: 'As!

JASON: 'Asn't!

PETER: 'As!

JASON: How do you know? You've never seen 'im!

PETER: I 'ave!

JASON: No you haven't, because, because he's been away for years and years and years and years!

PETER: Oh yeah, where is he then?

JASON: *(Pause)* He's a sailor, *and* he's sailing round the world, *and* he sends us postcards, see!

PETER: What's his ship called then?

(JASON frowns, but does not reply.)

PETER: *(Sneering)* You don't know do you? 'Cos he isn't a sailor on a ship!

JASON: Yes he is!

PETER: Well, what's it called then?

JASON: It's a great big cruiser ship, a liner, my Mum says.

PETER: Yeah, well what's it called?

JASON: It's called er, er . . . it's a long name.

PETER: You're making it all up. You don't know!

JASON: Yes I do! I'm just trying to remember.

PETER: Yeah, well, what's your Dad's great big ship called then?

JASON: I know! I know! It's called, er, it's called – HMS *Wormwood Scrubs*!

PETER: *(Pause)* Oh yeah, I've heard of that. Are you sure it's a ship?

JASON: Course it is.

PETER: *(Acknowledges end of battle because some sixth sense tells him it's time to start something else.)* OK Let's play 'Hide and Seek' then.

JASON: All right. *(He starts to recite, pointing to himself and to Peter on each word. He starts by tapping his own chest on the word 'Itsy'.)*

Itsy – Bitsy
Barney – Blue
I – T
Spells – It
That's – You!

You're 'It', OK? I'll start counting to ten and then I'm coming.

PETER: *(Runs off shouting.)* Close your eyes!

JASON: *(Closes his eyes and counts.)* One, two, three, four, five, six . . . *(Pauses, and opens his eyes.)* Course it's a ship! *(Closes his eyes.)* . . . six, seven, eight, nine, ten! COMING!

Lights fade, curtain falls, or blackout on 'COMING!'
Music: 'Girls and Boys Come Out to Play'.

A Particular Star

This Nativity Play requires a disciplined chorus of actors for the narration, who, when not narrating, become passengers reading newspapers, knitting, dozing, etc. The chorus speech arrangements indicated in the stage directions are suggested forms, directors should feel free to experiment.

The play takes place on a ferry-boat. The Mersey River was originally envisaged, the crossing between Liverpool and Birkenhead, but it could be any river.

The scenery could be a composite set of a ferry-boat in cross-section, revealing four areas, a railed deck area, an outside seating area, a small passageway, and a saloon. Alternatively it could be simply four acting areas defined by lighting alone, with rostra and props used to suggest the scene. When a scene is taking place in one area the lights are either very dim or killed altogether in the other areas.

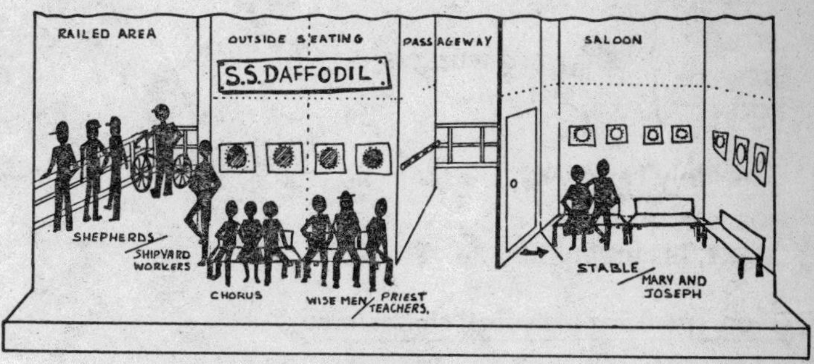

Sound effects can be homemade recordings or taken from sound-effect discs available through record shops. Several companies produce these records, notably BBC Enterprises Ltd.

NB The 'Eerie' noise. This can be achieved by plucking the string of a guitar, bass or violin and then tightening the string at the peg, producing a 'poi-y-ying' sound. Or you could invent your own 'Eerie' sound.

CAST

SEAMAN 1
SEAMAN 2
The CHORUS: Four or more voices, male and female
VOICE 1
VOICE 2
VOICE 3
VOICE 4

The Three Wise Men

PETER FARRELL, a teacher
FATHER MACCARTHY, a priest
EUGENE KALASHEWSKY, *(Kala-shef-ski)* a Polish refugee

The Shepherds

TOM
PHIL
GERARD
JOHN
} shipyard workers

The Holy Family

JOE, a carpenter
MARY, his pregnant wife

Non-speaking historical characters

ST PETER
MOSES
GOOD POPE JOHN
MARTIN LUTHER
NELSON

Other historical characters could be added, just for fun, provided it is conceivable that they might be members of the Church Triumphant! Conversely the cast could be reduced by having a narrator instead of a chorus, and the shepherds could be reduced to two.

The curtain rises slowly, lights are faded up slowly, to about half the full lighting. At the same time the sound effects build up slowly, water lapping against wood, seagulls, foghorns, creaking hawsers and timbers, ferry-boat engines humming. The CHORUS *are seated on the 'outside' seating. For the moment they are passengers, reading newspapers, knitting, talking, etc.*

SEAMAN: *(At the railed deck.)* All aboard! Clear the gangway!

(Eerie noise – Poi-y-ying!)

The lights fade out in all areas and then focus on the CHORUS, *who, one by one, emerge from their passenger characters when required to speak their verse.*

VOICE 1: It's never quiet here, on the river,
not with tugboats snorting and tooting,
yapping at the heels of great bull liners
who rumble their rebuke, so deep
you feel it in your boots.
Not what you would call quiet,
this squealing and screaming,
this endless accusation of gulls
squabbling for crumbs
from a pensioner's crumpled bag.

(Eerie noise – Poi-y-ying!)

VOICE 2: Sucking tide and creaking
wire-spliced hawser
fight for possession of the ferry.

The trembling shiver of the landing-stage
draws your gaze
to the cracks between the boards.
The lap, slap, lapping of sea green
melancholy water
sings a lament for sailors,
fathoms beneath your feet,
and you cannot say it's quiet, on the river.

(Eerie noise – Poi-y-ying!)

VOICE 3: The ferry-boat is noisy
loud with dreams and drama.
A ten-minute voyage is all that is needed
for lovers to seal their fate for a lifetime;
for children to circumnavigate the world;
for pin-striped adventurers to bid farewell
to the security of nine 'til five
and toss their Filofax diaries
into the waves.

(Ship's bell – tings twice. Lights come up on the passageway.)

FATHER MACCARTHY *enters and goes to the railed area.* PETER FARRELL *enters and sits on the 'outside' seating.* EUGENE KALASHEWSKY *enters and walks to the downstage side of the railed area and gazes out.* JOE *and* MARY *also enter through passageway and stand facing the audience gazing out over the river, and whispering to each other. The shipyard workers begin to gather at the upstage end of the passageway. As soon as the ship's bell tings, and whilst the other characters are making their entrance,* CHORUS VOICE 4 *speaks.*

VOICE 4: They are boarding the ferry now.
Nightshift workers beginning another day
in their topsyturvy lives.
Women in head scarves and rollers.
And quiet Mary from the Dingle
with her secret that everyone can see,
leans on the arm of the man who trusts her.

(Eerie noise – Poi-y-ying! and water churned by propeller screw.)

VOICE 1: In clerical black, Father MacCarthy
stares at mud-brown swirling water
and rehearses sermons
he would never dare preach;
of children neglected
not in some famine-stricken dust bowl
but in his parish;
of the old and hungry
living on water-biscuits and memories,
not proud, but too ashamed
to admit to poverty.

VOICE 2: Chalk-sleeved Peter Farrell
sighs and ticks the blotched
scrawling essays
of the ink-fingered Lower Fifth,
and wonders if Lewis J.
has the makings of a poet.

A bicycle bell rings and the shipyard workers, talking and laughing, make their way from the passageway, around the back of the 'outside' seating area and emerge into the railed area, upstage.

FATHER MACCARTHY *and* EUGENE KALASHEWSKY *find seats next to* PETER FARRELL.

VOICE 3: Laughing, Tom and Phil
and Peter and Gerard
with red, lead-stained caps
have pushed bicycles up the gangway,
glad to have finished another shipyard day.

VOICE 4: Old Eugene,
who remembers Poland before the war,
has not seen the deck beneath his feet
nor tasted the salt
in the onshore breeze.
His world is now so small.

All his triumphs and tragedies
age in suitcases and trunks,
campaign medals, yellow photographs,
souvenirs of youth in an era erased
by the march of ideologies.
All he was and is
in a terraced house
with swords on the wall, and tapestry
woven with dreams of home.

SEAMAN 1: *(In railed area.)* All gone aft!
SEAMAN 2: *(Offstage)* All gone for'ard!

(Ship's bell clangs. Three blasts on foghorn, for ferry reversing.)

VOICE 1: Gangplanks are drawn up,
lines are cast off,
and zephyrs from the sea
caress the passengers.
For some there is gaiety
in the ferry's lifting decks,
and yet others
sense the mystery in her wake.

(Eerie noise – Poi-y-ying!)

VOICE 2: But no one is aware that tonight
is the night it happens.
Tonight, fact and fiction,

VOICE 3: reality and myth,

VOICE 4: history and future,

ALL: fuse.

Tonight, under the stars,
over the noisy water,
it happens.

(Eerie noise – Poi-y-ying!)

VOICE 3: Tonight,
under a particular star,
somewhere in the middle of the river,
time stops.

VOICE 1: Only for a millionth part of a second,
but eternity is contained
in a fraction of a moment,
eternity, and all creation.

VOICE 2: Good Pope John will link arms
with Luther, his separated brother.

VOICE 3: Nelson will nudge Peter
the fisherman of Christ.

VOICE 4: And Moses will watch God
moulding Adam from the clay.

(Eerie noise – Poi-y-ying!)

VOICE 4: Crossing the sky, like some ancient scroll,
history will unfold.
Commoners and kings
will tumble through the heavens,
heroes will march through a galaxy of days
and all the years will be lit
by this particular star.

The CHORUS *begin to recite a whispered rhythmical ticking sound.*

'A Tick Tock, A Tick Tock Tick
A Tick Tock, A Tick Tock Tick' etc.

The rhythmical ticking could be accompanied by finger clicking, VOICES *1 and 2 continue the rhythmical ticking and clicking whilst* VOICES *3 and 4 recite, very rhythmically.*

VOICES 3 and 4: There is no slow
and there is no fast,
there is no future

and there is no past;
the only time is here and now;
I can tell you that it happens
but I can't tell you how.

Under a star
there is time to kill
when the clocks all stop. *(Everybody freezes!)*
. . . and time . . . stands . . . still.

The people of tomorrow are on their way
with yesterday's men
and the leaders of today.
The fish in the sea
and the birds in flight
are waiting for the wonder
of what happens tonight.

Under a star . . . etc.

Tomorrow's child is born today
though he was living yesterday.
Before the darkness knew the light
his spirit was alive
and his word was bright.

Under a star . . . etc.

(Words, whispers and clicks all fade with the lights. In blackout throb of boat engines, seagulls, bow waves.)

Lights fade up on passageway and saloon to reveal JOE *and* MARY *outside the saloon.*

JOE: Here you are Mary, let's go inside. You can sit down and put your feet up. Are you all right, love?
MARY: I'm all right, I'm just tired, that's all.

(They enter the saloon. He is carrying bags.)

JOE: Try not to worry, love. I'm sure we'll find somewhere across the water. I don't care what it is. We'll have a roof over our head when the time comes, somehow.

MARY: *(She puts her hand on his arm.)* Joe, I'm not worried. I know it will be all right.

JOE: *(He puts the bags on the end of a seat.)* Let's sit here. *(They sit.)* Lean on me. That's the way.

(She closes her eyes and they sit in silence for a while. Her head is on his shoulder and he is stroking her hair, very gently.)

MARY: Joe?

JOE: Yes, love?

MARY: What made you decide – you know, about me?

JOE: *(He gives a little laugh.)* If I told you, you might think I was round the bend.

MARY: You know I won't think that. Tell me.

JOE: I just woke up one morning and knew.

MARY: Knew what?

JOE: Well, I woke up very suddenly. I'd been having one of those dreams, you know, the kind in which you seem to be falling, and you never reach the bottom. Well, usually you wake up from one of those dreams with a bit of a shock. But in this dream, I didn't reach the bottom because something stopped me. It was as if I were floating, drifting like a leaf falling from a tree. Only instead of going down, I started to go up, as if a great breath of wind was lifting me. It was wonderful. I didn't want it to stop. Honestly, it was out of this world, almost like one of those, er, what do they call them? 'Out of body' experiences. It was so peaceful. No, that's not right, *I* was peaceful, happy, incredibly happy. And suddenly I was awake and I knew. I knew it was going to be all right, with you and me. *(Laughs)* Does that sound – daft?

(Mary does not answer him immediately, she is trying to fit the pieces together. Eventually she speaks.)

MARY: Joe, this child, is – special. Oh I know that every child is special, but, Joe, I've wanted to tell you but, oh, it's even stranger than your dream. In fact I wasn't even asleep, it was more like a daydream really.

JOE: Well, you didn't laugh at my dream. I promise I won't laugh at yours.

MARY: I was at home. At my mother's, I mean. I was looking out of the window. The sun was streaming in. I couldn't remember ever having seen it so bright. The light seemed to fill the whole room. And then the glass started to dazzle me and I was about to turn away when I thought I saw a face, a man's face. I thought that it must be some kind of optical illusion because his face seemed to fill the entire window. I wanted to look away, but I couldn't. And I began to feel scared. It *was* a face. And it was looking at me. Then he spoke. He said, 'Don't be afraid, Mary.' I shut my eyes, but I could still see him. Then I heard him say, 'Mary, you are going to have a child, a wonderful child.' And I heard myself saying, 'That's not possible.' But he said, 'Your child will be the child of the Most High.' And I said, 'The Most High, what do you mean?' And the face smiled. It really was a beautiful face, almost too beautiful for a man. Then I said to myself, 'It's a dream, it isn't real.' But the beautiful face spoke again, he said, 'The shadow of the Most High will pass over you, and you will conceive a son, and your son will be the son of the Most High.' And then I said something strange. I said, 'I am a child of God, his servant. Whatever he wants of me, I'll do it.' The face smiled again, or at least it seemed to, and then the light became so bright that I closed my eyes. When I opened them, he'd gone. But there was a strange sound, like music but not quite. Joe, I've been hearing that sound ever since we boarded this ferry. I can still hear it.

(Eerie noise – Poi-y-ying!)

JOE: So can I. It's the sound that woke me from my dream.

(Poi-y-ying! Poi-y-ying! Poi-y-ying! Sea-wash, gulls crying. Lights fade to blackout.)

VOICE 1: Who tunes the ears
that hear the sounds
that spirits make?

VOICE 2: What notes pierce the traffic's roar,
the din of markets, money, and men?

VOICE 3: Why this carpenter, this fisherman, this dentist,
this lawyer, farmer, teacher, priest?

VOICE 4: Why him, why her, why me,
to hear the irresistible sound
of that small voice?

VOICE 1: How comes the deafness
of those who do not hear?
Are lives more wicked
or time more wasted?

VOICE 2: Which office-worker is measurably
more good than his fellow,
which steeplejack is nearer to God?

VOICE 3: Which baker moulds pastry
with a holier hand?

ALL: Do they choose
or are they chosen
to hear the whisper
that never dies?

Lights fade to blackout. Lights come up on railed deck area. The shipyard men are stacking their bicycles and joking with each other. During this scene the lights gradually change from normal colouring to an unusual colour so that everybody looks green, red or blue. The lighting could even begin to strobe.

GERARD: Eh! Watch it! I've got to ride that bike at the next Preston Guild!

TOM: What? That wreck? I wouldn't like to say that your bike was old, Gerry, but that ticket on the saddle says, 'Not To Be Used On Voyage. SS *Noah's Ark*'!

GERARD: Gerroff! Look at the wheels on your old wreck. Where did you get them, off a wagon-train?

TOM: They're good wheels them. They don't make 'em like that any more. Me Dad pinched them during the War.

PHIL: Who from? Kaiser Bill?

(Laughter)

JOHN: Hey! Fellers, look at that star!

PHIL: Yer what?

JOHN: Look, over there!

GERARD: Hey! Look at that! It's moving isn't it?

TOM: It's not a star. It's one of those things for the weather, you know, um, a satellite.

PHIL: That's not a satellite. It wouldn't be as bright as that. That's lighting up the whole sky.

(Poi-y-ying! Poi-y-ying! Poi-y-ying!)

As they are looking up, people in period costume, NELSON, GOOD POPE JOHN, *etc. come strolling on to the set. Some from upstage of railed area, some from the passageway. They are in incongruous pairs, some are talking but we hear no sound. Some stop and look up at the star. When the present-day people look at them, the period people are unconcerned and carry on as if the present-day people do not exist.*

JOHN: What's that? Can you hear a funny noise?

(Poi-y-ying! Eerie sounds occur throughout this scene.)

TOM: (*Nudges Phil and speaks,* sotto voce.) Eh! Phil! Don't look now, but there's a lot of funny people standing behind us.

GERARD: Hey! That old feller looks like Moses.

JOHN: How would you know what Moses looks like?

GERARD: Ah shurrup!

PHIL: That feller looks like Good Pope John, and who is he talking to?

JOHN: There's one over there with a fishing-net over the side. Look, him standing by that feller with the eye patch. He's supposed to be Nelson isn't he?

GERARD: Yeah. That's very good that. He's just like the pictures you see of him in books.

TOM: I'll tell you something else that's funny.

PHIL: What?

TOM: Nobody is taking a blind bit of notice of them. The passengers, they're just carrying on as if they couldn't see them. *(Shouts)* Hey, Mister! Who's that feller with the sword, standing next to you?

PASSENGER: *(Reading a newspaper, looks up, looks around, and sees nothing.)* Are you trying to be funny? Is it some kind of joke?

TOM: Sorry, Mister. Forget it. *(To the others.)* See what I mean?

(Eerie noise – Poi-y-ying!)

PHIL: There's that noise again, listen.

GERARD: It's got to be some kind of practical joke.

(Poi-y-ying! Poi-y-ying! Poi-y-ying! The sound of seagulls increases to very loud. Other eerie sounds could be added. For example, an 'oooing' choir. CHORUS *could hum some harmonising chord, or discord.)*

JOHN: Look at that star! It's right over the boat!

(By now the surreal lighting should have been achieved.)

TOM: Hey! Fellers! The boat's not moving! They've stopped the engines!

(Sea-wash and the cries of many seagulls. Plus atmospheric music building to a climax which is the (unseen) arrival of the angel Gabriel.)

JOHN: And look at the birds! Look at the gulls, there's hundreds of them, thousands!

PHIL: You can't see the sky for them! Hey! We're not the only ones who can see all this. Look at them over there!

During this scene, at the 'outside' seating area FARRELL, KALASHEWSKY *and* FATHER MACCARTHY *have indeed seen the strange events, but they have been more awestruck and remained speechless. They are standing and now begin to wander towards the railed area.*

FATHER MACCARTHY: Jesus, Mary and Joseph! I've never seen the likes of it in my entire life. *(He turns to Farrell.)* What do you make of it?

FARRELL: I don't know, Father, I don't know. It's so – it's so bizarre, unreal.

KALASHEWSKY: Or perhaps, Gentlemen, it is the beginning of reality.

FARRELL: The beginning of what?

KALASHEWSKY: Reality, real life. Don't you feel a curious sense of peace, of tranquillity?

FATHER MACCARTHY: With all this noise, and those birds?

PHIL: Excuse me. Have you noticed that the engines have stopped? We're not moving.

FARRELL: *(Looking over the side.)* You're right, there's no wake, nothing.

KALASHEWSKY: That's what I meant by peaceful, there are no mechanical sounds.

GERARD: But what about that lot over there? *(He points to passengers.)* I'd swear to God those people haven't noticed anything.

KALASHEWSKY: Why should they? Nothing has happened to them.

FARRELL: But something has happened, *is* happening.

KALASHEWSKY: Perhaps only to us, perhaps we are the only ones who have stopped.

TOM: And what about all these people in fancy dress?

FATHER MACCARTHY: They're not in fancy dress. They're real. And they're all speaking different languages. I've heard Italian, German and some kind of Hebrew.

JOHN: But they all seem to understand each other.
PHIL: Have you noticed that the birds are mainly over the saloon?
FATHER MACCARTHY: That's where it is all happening, whatever it is, it's in there.
FARRELL: How do you know?
FATHER MACCARTHY: I – I just know that's all.
GERARD: Look! That bird! Look! It's huge! It must be an albatross! Over there! On the upper deck!

(At this point the sound effects are on the verge of reaching their climax. Eerie noises, gulls, and particularly the music are coming to a peak.)

JOHN: It must be the biggest bird in the world! It's coming down on the boat!
KALASHEWSKY: It has landed, and it's not a bird.
TOM: It's a feller! No it's not, it's – oh, it can't be!

The music reaches its climax and everything stops, except for the sound of a few gulls.

The lights go down, but when near blackout has been reached, a warm coloured spotlight comes up slowly in the saloon to reveal MARY, JOE *and the swathed child she is now holding. They are absolutely still. It is a tableau of the holy family.*

Eventually the workmen and the wise men make their way to the saloon door, FATHER MACCARTHY *opens the door.*

FATHER MACCARTHY: Holy Mother of God!

The saloon lighting fades. The CHORUS *have now assembled in the railed area. If practicable, some could be sitting on the rail when the lights fade up in this area. The verses that follow can be arranged as a speech montage, in which the 'quotations' are overlaid, according to the director's judgment.*

Speech Montage

It's never quiet here, in the mind,
not in this vast storehouse
of all our days, 'Stand up boy!'

of images, voices, laughter,
of pain's intensity;
not with an army of experiences
tramping through the brain.

'What's for tea,
Mum?'

'By the left,
quick march.'

Even in our therapeutic sleep
doors open and shut.
In the labyrinth of memory
there are signposts,
symbols of the event.

'Do you take this
woman to be your
lawful wedded . . .'

A hand, a smile, a face,
a tree with snow-laden leaves
and we slip and slide
on a cerebral trip
to childhood.

(Troika bells)
'A snowman! Let's
build a snowman!'

Not what you would call quiet,
this crowded playground
of jumping, running thoughts
and questions,
playing hop-scotch
on the cobbles of conscience.

'Daddy, why did
God make wasps?'

All our days
from that first, blind, kicking
exit from the womb;
and earlier,
when ear was pressed to belly
to feel and hear
the jerk of embryonic life.

*(A newborn baby
crying.)*

'Who made God, Miss?'

And before that,
when did the moulding start?
When first did we hear
the voices of our mothers?
Where did we begin?
Where did we begin? *(softer and softer)*
Where did we begin?

'Where did we begin?'

Lights fade down on railed area – and up on saloon.

In the saloon

JOE: Mary. There are some people here who want to see the baby.

(MARY *smiles and nods her assent.)*

JOE: Come over here lads.

The SHIPYARD MEN *cross to where* MARY *is seated.* FARRELL, KALASHEWSKY *and* FATHER MACCARTHY *follow. When they reach* MARY, JOHN *squats down on his haunches,* PHIL *perches on the edge of a seat and others gather round.* TOM *and* PHIL *are on the outer edge of the group.*

GERARD: Christ!
TOM: *(Whispering)* What's the matter?
GERARD: Nothing.
TOM: What did you say that for?
GERARD: I thought – I think I'm going off me head, Tom. Just for a minute I thought, I thought . . .
KALASHEWSKY: You thought you were looking at the infant Christ.
GERARD: I hope you don't mind me asking, but who are you?
KALASHEWSKY: Eugene Kalashewsky, a refugee, from the East.
TOM: From the East? *(He chuckles.)* A Wise Man?
GERARD: How did you know what I was thinking?
KALASHEWSKY: Because it is true. The child is the infant Christ.
TOM: But that happened two thousand years ago. Do you mean it's happened again?
KALASHEWSKY: No. I think this is the first time.

(Poi-y-ying! Poi-y-ying! Boat engines.)

FARRELL: Listen. The engines, they've started again.

FATHER MACCARTHY *goes to the door and looks outside. And* TOM *and* GERARD *have turned, slightly, away from the group.*

TOM: What are we going to do?

GERARD: About what?

TOM: Well – I suppose there's nothing you can do if you're dead.

GERARD: Dead? I'm not dead, mate. I've never felt more alive.

FATHER MACCARTHY: The engines *have* started, and the people from the past have gone. It's all over.

PHIL: The baby is still here.

KALASHEWSKY: Of course he is, that is what Emmanuel means.

FARRELL: God with us.

KALASHEWSKY: Precisely.

(They turn to look back at the child. As they do the ship's bell clangs, and a seaman's voice shouts.)

SEAMAN 1: Stand clear of the gangway, please!

The lights fade, slowly, on the saloon and then fade up on the 'outside' seating area.

VOICE 4: On this river, time has stood still,
the infinite source of all creation
lies in the arms of a girl,
and the shock cleaves reality,
logic fights for a precarious foothold,
and all the clocks
hold their breath.

VOICE 2: How can He
who holds the universe
in the palm of his hand,
choose one of millions
of tiny, revolving planets
and walk its streets?

VOICE 3: On this ferry-boat
a child has been born,
a child who was born
before the beginning of time.

VOICE 1: And we who are formed by time,

VOICE 2: ordered by time,

VOICE 3: disciplined by time,

VOICE 4: aged by time,

VOICE 1: and, in the end,
found short of time,

VOICE 2: cannot see the eternal.

VOICE 3: Even when He who is love
puts on the cloak of time
flesh and blood,
we do not see.

VOICE 4: Time is too frail a prison for love.
Even when love takes a name
and breathes the short breath of humanity
we cannot face the immensity
of infinite love
cradled in the arms of a girl.

(The CHORUS *crosses to the railed area.)*

VOICE 3: But it's never quiet here,
outside of time.

VOICE 4: There is too much work to do.
Dying takes an eternity to perfect.

VOICE 1: To see clearly,

VOICE 2: to know as we are known,

VOICE 3: to plumb the depth of 'God with us',

VOICE 4: to probe the mystery of the measureless
needs 'time' without end.

VOICE 1: To die at three score and ten
is too late.

VOICE 2: Death should come before the grave,
so that voyagers might prepare
the suckling child that fights for breath
within the lives of dying men.

VOICE 3: No, it's never quiet here
outside of time.

VOICE 4: The cries of newborn men and women
fill the ageless space
as Christ is born, again,

VOICE 1: and again,

VOICE 2: and again,

VOICE 3: and again.

During the last verse some voices have begun the 'Tick Tock' sequence, and the finger clicking.

ALL: Under a star
there is time to kill
when the clocks all stop
and time stands still.

Tomorrow's child is born today,
though He was living yesterday,
before the darkness knew the light
His spirit was alive
and His word was bright.

Under a star
there is time to kill
when the clocks all stop
. . . and time . . . stands . . . still!

Blackout

ANGELS

In the 'Angel' scripts which follow, the first few introduce us to the world of Walliel and his 'Common or Guardian' Angels, but the majority deal directly with those situations which threaten family life or place children in danger. They could be interspersed in a programme designed to heighten people's awareness of those areas which are of special concern to the National Children's Home, or they could be performed just for the fun of it.

Walliel and the Recruits

In this scene WALLIEL *is dressed in cricket whites, shirt and trousers and white shoes.*

WALLIEL: *(Addresses audience.)* Hello, are you the new recruits? I'm Walliel, er – I'm an angel. *(Waits for reaction.)* Oh, dear. I know why you're all grinning. You don't think I *am* an angel, do you? Yes, well, that's because *you* think you would recognise an angel if you saw one. And, you're thinking, if he was an angel, he'd have wings, and he'd be, sort of hovering, a few feet above the ground, and, he'd have a halo, and a long white robe and he'd have an aura, a kind of golden glow all around him. Well, I'm afraid that's where you are wrong. Of course, you angel recruits will be getting proper lectures about all this, but I can tell you, angels can't just go around in wings and haloes whenever they feel like it. Oh, good heavens no. You have to have a chit, that's right, a wings-and-haloes chit.

You see, properly speaking, wings-and-haloes is an angel's ceremonial full-dress uniform. Oh yes, you have to see the Quartermaster Sar'nt Angel, and he ticks everything off.

Halo – angels for the use of – one!
Wings – angels for the use of – one pair!
Glory – for the shining around of – one blaze!

That's how they measure it, glory, a blaze per angel. You'll learn all about glory from Angel Raphael when your training starts.

And then there's choir practice. All angels sing in the Heavenly Host, the choirs invisible. I sing baritone. And that's another thing. I bet you thought that angel choirs were all sopranos. Cecil B. deMille thought that; mark you he knows better now, of course.

Anyway, as I was saying, wings and haloes are only for very special occasions. And if you do use wings and haloes down on earth, you'll find that most people can't see you anyway. You have to be very high up to make a full colour appearance on earth. You have to be an Archangel or something like that. It's not for the likes of us. Not that *you* might not make Archangel one day, if you keep your halo clean. But we all have to start somewhere, and we start off as Common or Guardian Angels.

Now when your Common or Guardian Angels are down on earth, we're usually in disguise, in mufti. People can be sitting alongside an angel and they wouldn't know. We don't go shouting our mouths off. Our job is to try and guide people by dropping little hints and suggestions, nudging people gently in the right direction. Of course, you can nudge, shove and kick some people and they still don't take any notice. They wouldn't recognise an angel if he stood in front of them with golden wings and a fiery sword! Still, we keep on trying.

Making people laugh is one of our jobs, I mean good clean innocent laughter. Now little devils, imps, they try to get people to sneer and be sarcastic. They like to hear a dirty laugh. Sniggering, that's what they like. But you can always tell when a Common or Guardian Angel is doing a good job when you hear people laughing at themselves rather than at someone else's expense.

Well, you'll learn about all these things in your training. Anyway I can't stop, I hope to get my wings this afternoon. I must say, I've been rather looking forward to this, because, with wings, when I take my leave, I'll be able to say,

'Must Fly! – Bye!'

Raphael and the Recruits

RAPHAEL *is an archangel, and his costume should reflect his high rank. He is attended by an angel sergeant whose costume should indicate his rank – perhaps three golden chevrons on his chest. When they enter,* RAPHAEL *is preceded by* SAR'NT ANGEL. *If it is possible for them to glide in, on suitably disguised roller-skates, so much the better.*

(Trumpet fanfare. Enter SAR'NT ANGEL *and* RAPHAEL. *The fanfare ends.)*

SAR'NT ANGEL: Angel recruits, pray silence for His Graciousness the Archangel Raphael!

(Trumpet fanfare. SAR'NT ANGEL *moves to one side and bows towards* RAPHAEL *who comes forward and returns the bow. The fanfare finishes and* RAPHAEL *opens his mouth to speak, but before he can get a word out there is another trumpet fanfare.* RAPHAEL *moves aside and waits patiently. The fanfare ends and* SAR'NT ANGEL *moves forward again.)*

SAR'NT ANGEL: Pray silence for His Graciousness, the Archangel Raphael!

(Another trumpet fanfare. Once again SAR'NT ANGEL *bows to* RAPHAEL *who returns the bow, the fanfare ends, and* RAPHAEL *prepares to speak, but again there is another trumpet fanfare)*

SAR'NT ANGEL: *(Turns to shout offstage.)* Trumpeters! Will you please . . .

RAPHAEL *holds up his hand to* SAR'NT ANGEL *who stops shouting.* RAPHAEL, *who has been serene and smiling throughout, makes a mystic gesture and the trumpets stop instantly.*

RAPHAEL: A splendid fanfare, Sar'nt Angel. A trifle too enthusiastic perhaps?

SAR'NT ANGEL: Sir!

RAPHAEL: Right, now gather round and pay attention please. My name, as you may know, is Raphael, second-in-command of the SIS, which stands for Spiritual Intelligence Services.

Now while you are here you will attend a Terrestrial Survival Course. You will learn about aliases and disguise. You will learn a hundred and fifty-seven ways of deterring, confusing and capturing the enemy, known to us as the DVLs, which is short for Damned, Vile and Lost spirits. You will learn how to code and decode messages, which in our trade are referred to as prayers. When you pass out as a CGA, that is, a Common or Guardian Angel, that will be one of your principal functions. Every day, every earth day that is, you will be expected to relay prayers from your charges to HQ. And at the end of the day, woe betide any angel who hasn't a prayer to his or her name.

Now, a word about 'glory'. Yesterday, which may be a few thousand earth years, but to us is merely the flap of a wing, yesterday, one of our angels in training, AC2 Walliel, that's Angel second class, which is the rank you will hold as soon as you are kitted out, Angel Walliel had been detailed to guide three wise men or kings to the stable at Bethlehem with strict orders to keep the kings well clear of Herod's Palace. Now he failed to do this, but ultimately redeemed himself by putting into the heads of the wise men the idea that they should leave the country by a different route.

Because of his preoccupation with the wise men, Angel Walliel also failed to join the Heavenly Choir for the ceremonial shining of glory all around, which meant that when he returned to HQ, he still had a completely unused supply of glory. The problem is, once glory has been issued it can never be returned to stores. Therefore, the Quartermaster Sar'nt Angel had no alternative but to instruct Angel Walliel to maintain custody of the issued glory and to use his initiative with regard to its release.

Angel Walliel decided that he would release a little glory whenever his charge on earth did a good deed or thought a good thought. This was considered by those on high to be rather a good idea. As a result there has been a change of standing orders in this regard. From now on, angels on guardian duty will carry a small supply of glory as part of their normal kit. Like Angel Walliel, some of you will be allocated a particular person to watch over on earth, the drill now is that whenever your charge does a kindness, listens to someone patiently, makes a sacrifice, rights a wrong, that sort of thing, then you will release a little glory to celebrate the fact. The release of small amounts of glory on earth has the additional benefit of causing confusion among devils for a short amount of earth time.

Well, we'll take a break there. You will find that the NAAFI is now open. Oh, for those of you who are very new, NAAFI stands for Nectar and Ambrosia For Inspiration canteen.

Right, Sar'nt Angel.

SAR'NT ANGEL: Sir!

RAPHAEL: Flap them out would you.

CURTAIN

(N.B. If this sketch is used before an interval be sure to have available, Nectar Tea, Ambrosia Coffee and of course, Angel Cake.)

Michael and the Recruits

MICHAEL *is the warrior angel and his costume should reflect this. His fanfare could be preceded by deep timpani beats. Enter a* SAR'NT ANGEL

SAR'NT ANGEL: *(Who addresses audience.)* Right! Angel recruits! Wings folding on parade follows the command, 'wings fold'. Then it's left over right, *silently!* I don't want to hear a flutter, right? Not the flutter of a single feather. OK. Let's try it. On the command! Wings! – Wait for it, wait for it – fold! Left over right, left over right! This is the Elysian Fields not Trafalgar Square! You're supposed to be a squadron of angels not a flock of flippin' pigeons! Right, now settle down. We've got a visit today from the old warrior himself, the Archangel Michael, commander-in-chief of the Heavenly Host. He'll be here any minute now, so I want you to . . .

(Timpani drum beats & fanfare.)

Stand by, here he is!

(Flash of lights – possibly a thunder flash.)

Archangel Michael, Sir! Angel recruits, this is Archangel Michael, commander-in-chief of . . .

MICHAEL: *Thank* you Sar'nt Angel. There's no need to hover angels, just pull up a cloud and float easy for a few minutes.

Now as you know, several earth millennia ago a celestial battle was fought in which the former Prince of Angels, Lucifer and, sadly, a great number of his followers, were cast out of Heaven. Now if Lucifer had not been blinded by pride and vanity he would have seen that the result was inevitable. Cast from Heaven he fell into the outer darkness and eventually made his way to the planet Earth, where initially he took the form of a serpent. He now adopts many guises. On earth, or anywhere else for that matter, neither he nor his followers can survive in the face of sacrificial love, or in the light of goodness. The sight of either forces him to retreat once more into the outer darkness. So, those are the chief weapons against evil – love and goodness. Lucifer is aware of the incredible love that the Almighty has for mankind, so he does his best to drag as many people as possible into his own dark and miserable kingdom.

His principal method is to persuade people that the gateway called 'Death' leads to the end of all experience. The end of love, laughter, the end of existence – oblivion. This is, of course, a huge double bluff. As the Prince of Darkness knows only too well, 'Oblivion' is actually one of the sinister prisons of his own kingdom.

Death Gate is not the end, in fact it is neither the beginning nor the end, it is simply a gate. It is true that you need light to find the path to Heaven; stumble through that gate in Lucifer's darkness and Oblivion and worse yawns before you.

But the Son of God has opened that gate, and a great beacon of love lights up the eternal road to the light and love of God. Indeed, the only way Lucifer can make people believe there is no light at that gate, is to get them to approach it with their backs to the light and with his horny hands clasped over their eyes, or in other words, blind them with cynicism and despair, long before they reach the gate.

He is a tenacious worker and is prepared to spend years gradually reducing people's sensitivity to love and truth. He does this by encouraging selfishness. Not in a big way. But little by little, and in time, the self-centred people graduate to meanness and then bitterness. Eventually they carp at everything and everyone, then they begin to find fault even in those who are closest to them, those who perhaps once they loved. Ultimately, the arrogance that Lucifer has been building up erupts in sneers at the nature of love itself.

As Common or Guardian Angels your job is to help people to grow in love, to encourage them to think the best, to say and do the best and believe with all their hearts that things will work for good for those who love God. One of your chief weapons will be a sense of the ridiculous.

The Devil wants people to take themselves seriously, to be *preoccupied* with self, how they feel, what other people think about them, to begin thinking that they can trust nobody except themselves. The Devil hates the laughter, of love. It is like the sun bursting through cloud, a meteor shower, a firework fountain whose chuckling sparks send Lucifer scurrying for the shadows.

In a word, your job is to help people towards the light of the love of God, dazzlingly displayed in the life, death and resurrection of Jesus Christ. And if you think that is fighting talk, well, what do you expect from an old warrior like me?

Carry on Sar'nt Angel. *(He steps aside and* SAR'NT ANGEL *steps forward.)*

SAR'NT ANGEL: Angel recruits! Wings! – wait for it, wait for it! – Fold!

(The SAR'NT ANGEL *and* MICHAEL *bow to each other as the curtain falls)*

Gabriel and the Graduate Recruits

GABRIEL *is Head of Heaven's PR department. Principal harpist and Head of 'vision dispatches'. He is charming, a heavenly prince, not unlike the Prince of Wales perhaps, but not* too *like! Although* GABRIEL *continues to address the audience as angel recruits, there are several angels, including* WALLIEL *sitting on stage on chairs designated for 'graduates'. When the curtain rises, or the lights fade up, the* SAR'NT ANGEL *is pacing up and down, and the* GRADUATES *are talking quietly amongst themselves. Harp chords are struck as* GABRIEL *enters. He is preceded by an angel (or several if cast and costumes are available) carrying scrolls – diplomas for the graduates. The graduates stand as* GABRIEL *enters. If the budget runs to it, other angels could be holding a canopy over* GABRIEL, *or perhaps one angel holding a large, suitably covered umbrella. The* SAR'NT ANGEL *is standing by the graduates. The procession comes to a halt. If there are several angels preceding* GABRIEL *they should form a guard of honour.* GABRIEL *steps out from under canopy/umbrella and holds out his hand to see if it is raining, he discovers it isn't and smiles.*

GABRIEL: *(To audience.)* Well, it's better to be safe than sorry, don't you think? And there *are* one or two clouds in Heaven with a rather skittish sense of humour. *(He sees the standing graduates.)* Oh, please do sit down. This is a very informal and happy occasion. We don't want to stand on ceremony, do we? *(He looks round at escort and canopy and smiles.)* Well, not very much anyway. *(Turns to audience.)* I say, it's awfully nice to meet new angel recruits. I don't think we've met have we? I'm Gabriel, Archangel and all that sort of rot. I'm actually responsible for Heavenly PR and the Visions and

Inspiration Dispatch Department, when they can drag me away from my harp.

I say, I don't suppose any of you are harpists are you? No? No, well I didn't expect you would be. You know we don't get many harpists coming up from Earth – trumpeters by the dozen, but hardly ever a harpist. Though I must say harps are awfully difficult to take to parties, don't you think?

Now, what was I saying? Oh, yes. My department deals, primarily, with the delivery of messages, dreams, visions and inspiration from Heaven to Earth. I am answerable directly to the HS, the Holy Spirit.

You could say that I am the velvet glove, whereas the Archangel Michael is more the iron fist. For instance, Michael's full dress uniform for earthly appearances includes a face like lightning, eyes like flaming torches, arms and legs burnished bronze, his body is crystal and his voice is like the roar of a multitude; which is all very well if you want to put the fear of God into somebody. Indeed it was a squad of angels from Michael's department who were sent to roll away the stone from the tomb. Not surprisingly, the soldiers guarding the tomb simply passed out on sight of them. But that is not quite the right style for my department's work. In fact our job is usually about putting people at their ease. My last visit to Earth was to Nazareth, to inform the BVM of her role in Operation Nativity.

Again, it was angels briefed by my department who greeted Mary Magdalene and the women outside the tomb on the Day of Resurrection, to inform them of JC's position at that time. They were rather inexperienced angels, they were supposed to be gardeners, but earthly gardeners, dressed in white? My fault I'm afraid, I should have told them that on Earth they simply do not have the same facilities that we have for making things white and removing stains. If you see what I mean.

Actually angels are very rarely called upon to make public appearances. *(He waves an elegant hand toward the graduates.)* You, my friends, will be sent to Earth as Guardian Angels. For most of the time you will either be invisible to humans or you will be disguised to look like someone who is known to the person you are guarding. In your invisible role, your task is to whisper positive and encouraging ideas into the ears of your charges.

Now this brings me to the main purpose of this gathering. Speech Days and Graduation Ceremonies can be so full of words that although they might be very enjoyable occasions it's often very hard to remember anything that was said. So, I want you to remember only one thing, and it is this. When people have difficult decisions to make the guidance rule for all Guardian Angels is as follows, 'The right thing to do, in any situation, is always the most loving thing that can be done.' Perhaps I'd better say it again, just to be sure. 'The right thing to do, in any situation, is always the most loving thing that can be done.'

Don't forget, the deciding battle has been won, once and for all on Calvary. However, Lucifer is a poor loser, and he and his imps and demons are creeping about down there trying to drag people's minds towards negative things, sins against love, revenge, thinking the worst and his most destructive weapon, despair. Your task is to inspire, by whatever means you can, reconciliation, thinking the best and above all, hope and optimism. And now Sar'nt Angel, would you call out the names of today's graduate angels, thank you.

SAR'NT ANGEL: *(Bows to* GABRIEL.*)* Sir. I present to you Graduate Guardian Angel Tessiel.

TESSIEL *comes forward, is presented, and the kind of* sotto-voce *conversation that is usual on these occasions ensues. She takes her diploma and returns to her seat. The same ritual is followed by however many graduates there are in the cast. The last graduate should be* WALLIEL. *All angel names end in -el or, -iel –* GABR-IEL, MICHA-EL, RAPHA-EL, WALL-IEL, TESS-IEL, *and so on. Angels who are referred to in other scripts include,*

RACHAEL, PAMMIEL *and* TOMMIEL. *You can have as many as you like. When the ceremony is finished,* GABRIEL *addresses the audience once more.*

GABRIEL: Now, I actually have a commission to issue today. It is to Guardian Angel Walliel. *(*WALLIEL *stands.)* Walliel, I believe that you have been trained in London speech patterns. Which areas in particular?

WALLIEL: *(Doing the accent.)* Norf Sir, Totten'am, Wood Green, 'Arringey, Finsbury Park, Camden Town and uvver boroughs norf o'Regents Park. Sir!

(Walliel could, of course, be given any local dialect)

GABRIEL: Oh, I say, that's very good! When we leave will you come with me, and I will brief you in detail. Finally, let me repeat my message, so that if anyone asks you, what was Gabriel's message, you will be able to say, 'the right thing to do, in any situation . . . *(He waves towards the graduates.)*

GRADUATES: . . . is always the most loving thing that can be done.'

GABRIEL: Wonderful. And now I must get back to the harpists' rehearsal. Are you sure that none of you are harpists? No? Ah well, Oh! *(He looks up.)* Is that rain? *(There is a crash of thunder and* GABRIEL *wags a disapproving finger at the clouds.)* Don't you dare! *(Another crash of thunder.)* Come on everybody! Run for it! They won't take any notice of me! *(To Audience)* Bye!

(There is another crash of thunder and the graduation party scatters as the curtain descends.)

In the following eight scenes, featuring the Angel WALLIEL, *all stage directions and suggestions for music are the same.* WALLIEL *should appear dressed as an angel, with or without wings according to wardrobe ingenuity. His performances could be introduced by some harp music, or perhaps a non-vocal version of a song popularly known as 'You may not be an angel' (the correct title is 'I'll string along with you'.) Whatever music is chosen should become* WALLIEL'*s 'signature tune', and be played on his entrance and at the end of each scene.*

As the lights fade up, Angel WALLIEL *enters and strides downstage to address his recruits – the audience.*

Walliel and the Wilmots (1)

WALLIEL: 'Ello. Do you remember me? I'm Walliel, AC2 Walliel, Angel second class, Common or Guardian Angel. My charges are all asleep down there, so I thought I'd pop up for a few Earth seconds just to let you angel recruits know 'ow I'm getting along. I've been temporarily assigned to Johnny Wilmot, resident of Wood Green, London N.22. You see I'm a relief Guardian Angel at the moment. I'm giving Angel Tommiel a chance to take a spot of well-earned leave.

You probably didn't know that all Guardian Angels are trained in the speech patterns of whoever they're looking after. Well, you 'ave to, see, or you might not understand what they're talking about. I mean it's not just accents and dialects, it's languages as well. I mean I'm just as likely to be sent to Russia as I am to England, or the Isle of Tonga for that matter.

Nah then, Johnny Wilmot isn't a bad lad, but he's

inclined to be a bit selfish, well, thoughtless really, though it adds up to the same thing in the end. For instance, his wife, Joan, spends all of her day looking after their two small children. Nah, when Johnny gets home from work he doesn't help a lot. In fact, now that the pubs are open all day he's started popping into the local for a drink on the way home. I'm afraid the ever open pub is proving a bit of a temptation for a lot of people.

Anyway, as far as Johnny is concerned it now means that by the time he gets home the children have gone to bed, so he doesn't see much of them. Then after his meal, when Joan is doing the ironing and she wants to talk, Johnny just sits in front of the television, and what with a day's work and a couple of pints, he just falls asleep. Which isn't a lot of fun for Joan. You see, the real trouble is, a couple of Lucifer's little imps have got a firm grip on some of Johnny's mates. I mean, I can recognise their voices, when they speak through his friends. They say things like, 'Come on Johnny, a man's entitled to a drink.' And I whisper in his ear, 'What about Joan?' But the gremlins jump in with, 'Who wears the trousers in your house then Johnny? Come on, you're *entitled* – what are yer, man or mouse?' So I whisper, 'What about the kids?' And the gremlins say, 'Just a quickie won't do any harm.'

Well, it's been going on like that ever since I took over. But the other day I spoke to Tessiel. Now she is Guardian Angel for Johnny's Mum, who's just got a job as a tea-lady in an office which is almost next door to the pub where Johnny drinks. In fact Tessiel says that his mother usually comes out of the offices just two minutes after Johnny has gone into the pub. So I said, 'Does she know?' And Tessiel said, 'No, but if you want, I'll try and get her to come out at the same time as he is going in and . . .' 'Of course,' I said. 'They'll meet and with any luck he'll give her a lift home.' Now, I'll say this for Johnny, there's nothing he wouldn't do for his old Mum. Well, it worked out better than I had hoped. In fact Tessiel must have been working overtime 'cos Johnny's Mum not only went home with Johnny for a cup of tea but, after she had helped put the children to bed, she said, 'Why don't you and Joan pop out to the pictures or something? It would give Joan a bit of a break. I'll look after the kids.'

Of course, Guardian Angels can't shake hands when they're on duty, but have you ever seen two invisible angels wink at each other? Well, I don't suppose you have, but they do you know. – Eh! Just a minute! (*He looks down over the edge of the stage.*) One of the kids is stirring. I'd better be off. Tata for now then. See yer! (*He exits.*)

(Music plays as the lights fade.)

Walliel and the Wilmots (2)

WALLIEL: 'Ello, Angel Walliel reporting back from his temporary assignment as Guardian Angel to Johnny Wilmot of Wood Green, London. Now I've been working on Johnny, trying to get him to be more involved with his kids. Since he missed going to the pub a couple of times his friends have stopped asking him, in fact their little tempting devils are busy trying to get their claws into some other poor soul. Which is fine as far as Johnny is concerned, but somebody else's poor old Guardian Angel must be working overtime now.

My problem with Johnny is, he thinks that he can't cope with the kids, and he can really, or at least he could if he put his mind to it. Well, I thought I'd try and help things along a bit. The other night when Joan was putting the kids to bed, I sent a message to HQ requesting help from another locally based Guardian

Angel. My request was granted, because just as Joan was fastening up the second lot of pyjama buttons, the phone rang. Johnny answered it and said, 'Joan, it's for you, love. It's your sister, Helen.' Joan said, 'Oh, look love, see to the kids will you?'

That phone call was the result of some hard work on the part of Helen's Guardian Angel, Pammiel. Well, that's when I really got to work. I kept whispering in Johnny's ear, 'A story, tell them a story.' I saw him looking at the children, and then he looked at Joan, and that was all right, 'cos she'd settled down to a good old chinwag with her sister. So again I whispered, 'A story, tell them a story.'

Well, I nearly sang a triple Alleluia when I heard him say, 'Would you like Daddy to tell you a story?' The kids jumped up and down on their beds and Johnny sat down with them and began, 'Once upon a time . . .' Actually he's a very good storyteller, made it up as he went along, I got quite caught up in it myself. The trouble was he didn't know how to finish it. But that gave me a brilliant idea! I kept whispering in his ear, 'Part two, tomorrow. Part two tomorrow!' And it worked! The next night Johnny carried on with the story, only this time Joan was sitting with the kids as well!

So, things are coming along quite well in Wood Green. I have had some complaints from Raphael, mainly due to the fact that Johnny never sends any prayers to HQ. So I'm working on the children's Guardian Angels to get the children to ask their Dad to say a 'Good night prayer'. It hasn't happened yet – but I'm working on it. Well, I'd better fly. An angel's work is never done. Bye! *(He exits.)*

(Music plays as the lights fade.)

Walliel and Jack

WALLIEL *and the* SAR'NT ANGEL *appear in this scene.*

WALLIEL: 'Ello, Guardian Angel Walliel reporting back to HQ. I'd better bring you up to date. Well, until recently I was temporary relief Guardian Angel to Johnny Wilmot of Wood Green in London. I'm happy to say that Johnny has managed to shake off some very nasty little devils who had been trying to get their claws into him. Angel Tommiel is back on duty in the Wilmot household and he is delighted with Johnny's progress. Now you know what it's like. You have a little success in a particular area and you get pigeon-holed. Though 'pigeon-holed' isn't quite right for an angel somehow. I wonder what the right expression is? Angel-slotted? Ah well, never mind. The long and short of it is, when I got back to the Elysian Fields, which is where the angels' HQ is, the Sar'nt Angel popped round to see me and he said . . .

SAR'NT ANGEL: *(enters from wings, carrying a clipboard)* Angel Walliel.

WALLIEL: He said.

SAR'NT ANGEL: You'll be pleased to know that you have been mentioned in dispatches. Johnny Wilmot has said to his wife, on several occasions, 'I think my Guardian Angel has been working overtime, thank God.' You can't hope for a better mention in dispatches than that, lad. Apart from anything else, that's the nearest Johnny Wilmot has got to saying a prayer for a long time. The Archangel Gabriel has a special assignment for you. You are to report to his office for a full briefing. Oh, and before you go over to his office, put your halo straight laddie, you're an angel, not a spitfire pilot! And er, well done Walliel, keep up the good work. *(He exits.)*

WALLIEL: Well, to cut a long story short, the Archangel

Gabriel has given me a special assignment to children in danger. He gave me a list of six special cases. Now they've all got Guardian Angels, but I was being sent as an emergency back-up. This is often done when there seems to be special need. Of course, even if you sent a whole squadron of angels, it mightn't make any difference, you can't make people do good or bad. In the end, they have to decide that for themselves. All we can do is keep pointing out the right path and hope that they will take it. But in the case of children, very often they can be set a long way down the wrong path for no fault of their own. I mean you can't put a lot of blame on a four-year-old, can you?

Like my first little lad, Jack, he's only four years old, but he's a right little tearaway! He lives in Deptford, and he's the terror of the NCH Family Centre. When he isn't screaming the place down, he's either pulling another kid's hair or pouring custard on his own. And, according to the lady at the Centre, he has an uncanny knack of finding the most inconvenient places to stick his plasticine. But mostly, he just yells. Now, he hasn't got a Daddy; well, of course he has, but he's just never seen him. It might sound obvious, but I reckon that's the problem. So, I'm working on Chris, the milkman who delivers to the Family Centre. He's a nice cheery sort of chap, and he brings the milk right into the nursery classroom, every morning at about ten o'clock. Of course by that time, Jack the Lad has got more poster paint in his hair than on his paper, and more likely than not there's the best part of a currant bun stuck in his ear.

So, today, I did a bit of angelic nudging, just as Chris the milkman was passing young Jack. I don't really know what I was hoping for, but I think we've made a start. Chris looked at little Jack and said, 'What are you painting, Sunshine?' Then he bent down, pulled the bun out of his ear and ruffled his hair. Jack sized up the milkman (they're good at that, children,) then he stuck his finger in his ear, to compensate for the missing bun, and blew a very noisy raspberry. 'Ere,' says the milkman. 'I tell yer what, do us a drawing of your Mum, and tomorrow you can show it to me, right?'

Just then I got an emergency call from the Guardian Angel of another child, so I had to fly off. But when Jack's Mum came to collect him, the Family Centre lady said, 'He's been as good as gold today, and he's done ever such a lot of drawings.'

I'd better be around tomorrow when the milkman calls. You know, we Guardian Angels are not supposed to be match-makers, but, well, you never know where this could lead! *(He looks down, over the edge of the stage.)* 'Ere, that Big Ben is usually right, isn't he? Doesn't Earth time fly? So must I. Bye! *(He exits.)*

(Music plays as the lights fade.)

Walliel and the Girl Who Kept Falling Down

WALLIEL: The trouble with being a Guardian Angel is that you can't touch. You can't physically touch people. Sometimes I long to hold them, or hug them, or catch them when they fall, but I can't, it's not allowed. You see, Jane kept falling down. Clumsy and awkward, she kept breaking things. 'Accident prone' they called it. When I was briefed it was suggested that I should think very carefully about her parents. Well, it didn't take long to discover what was at the root of Jane's clumsiness. Every day Jane came home from school, opened the kitchen door and there they were, at it hammer and tongs, rowing, shouting, right up and downers, every day. It's not surprising really. Jane's Dad has been out of work for ages, and it's a struggle to make ends meet, in fact usually they don't – meet that is.

I keep hearing people say, 'You don't have to be rich to be happy, so long as you've got your health and strength, that's all that matters.' Trouble is, if you haven't got any money you are not likely to be very healthy. If you are in a constant state of anxiety, rows and fights come all too easily. No, you don't have to be rich, but you do need to be able to pay the bills, if you can't, you don't stay healthy long.

Jane's Dad had been out of work so long that he'd almost given up hope. Now that is when a Guardian Angel has his work cut out, 'cos there is nothing the Devil likes better than people giving up hope. He had stopped looking at the job vacancies down at the Job Centre. He hadn't got a trade. Over the years he'd done all sorts of odd jobs, a bit of labouring on a building site, been a night watchman at a factory, and tried his hand at furniture removing, but nothing ever lasted. He was a kind of square peg that had seen a lot of round holes.

And talking about round holes, that's where hope has come alive for Jane's Dad. Cos, it was a hole, a round hole, in the road, that Jane managed to put her foot in, and twist her ankle very painfully, right outside her own front door. Poor Jane, her Dad wasn't very sympathetic, but her Mum said, 'You'll have to take her down to the casualty, I've got the baby and everything.' Well, down at the hospital they had to wait for ages. The nurses were run off their feet. Jane's Dad had to find a wheelchair for her 'cos there wasn't anyone free to fetch one for her. Then an old man came in, hobbling. He needed a chair to take him to X-Ray, and the poor nurse had to say, 'I'm sorry love, you'll just have to sit on a bench in the waiting room until there's a porter free.'

Jane's Dad was just sitting staring into space, so I whispered in his ear, 'Get the old man a chair, you know where they are.' And suddenly, Jane's Dad said,

'I'll get a chair, Nurse.' The nurse said, 'Will you? That's good of you. Thank you very much.' It was becoming very clear what I had to do, so I kept up the pressure. When Jane's Dad got back with the chair, I kept whispering in his ear, 'Ask the nurse about porters, ask, ask!' I thought he was never going to get the message, but in the end he did. I saw the thought flicker across his face and then he said, 'Are you short of porters then, Nurse?' 'Short?' she said, 'We're not only short, we've got three off sick!'

Well the long and short of it is, Jane's Dad is now a temporary relief hospital porter. It's only temporary of course, but he's taken to it like a duck to water. He loves every minute of it. Taking food round the wards, delivering patients to X-Ray and the theatre, or taking someone out for a bit of fresh air. He does quite a bit of laughing too, there's a lot of humour in a hospital. I've got a feeling they'll keep him on. I think they can see that he's a square peg who's found his niche, if you know what I mean. And the difference it's made at home! Funny thing, Jane's ankle seemed to get better in no time. When she gets home from school, there's no rowing. And when her Dad gets home he's full of stories about the hospital. Added to which, Jane hasn't fallen down, or dropped a plate for weeks now! I can't say, 'And they all lived happily ever after', because life's not like that. But there's hope, and that's always a setback for the Devil. *(Looks down over edge of stage.)* Oh. Look, that Big Ben is striking again! Must fly. Bye! *(He exits.)*

(Music plays as the lights fade and the curtain falls.)

Walliel and Benji the Dreamer

WALLIEL: I suppose you know I'm wearing my wings out flitting from one child in trouble to the next. Well, that's what this tour of duty is about, children in danger. The Sar'nt Angel hinted that I might get made up to LACG if I did well on this assignment. That's Leading Angel, Common or Guardian. But I'm not so sure that it will happen, not on this assignment anyway.

You know, ninety-nine times out of a hundred, if a child has got problems, his number one problem is usually his Dad, or his Mum, or the *lack* of Mum or Dad. Like Benji. You see Benji is a big talker, a liar, a boaster. He'll say anything to get attention, 'cos that's what he wants, well, not just attention, what he really wants is love. Not a lot, just a little would do the trick. Perhaps 'liar' is too strong a word. Dreamer would be more accurate, yes that's it, Benji the Dreamer. His Mum and Dad are ever so well off. He's 'something in the City' and she is an area manageress for a group of shops. Benji's friends don't know that, 'cos he's told them that his Dad is a test pilot and his Mum is a film star. At least they were a few weeks ago. I think the latest is that his father is doing something very secret for the government and his Mum, when she's not making films with Dustin Hoffman, is very heavily involved in gold smuggling for the Mafia. As Benji says, 'She's Sicilian, on her mother's side.' Actually, her mother was born and bred in Peckham and the nearest she's ever been to Sicily is a day trip to Calais, and that was organised by a very sinister organisation known to the brotherhood as the Peckham Co-op.

The trouble is he is on his own so much. A variety of ladies he calls 'Auntie' spend the evening in his home while his parents are attending this or that association dinner, or going to the theatre or the ballet or trying out a 'marvellous new wine bar' where the cook is said to have worked at Buckingham Palace. So, Benji lives in a world of fantasy. Nearly all his fantasies are about his mother and father. On the few occasions when he does see his Mum and Dad, they are always in a hurry, always just going out, always saying, 'Not now, darling. Tell me about it tomorrow. Be good for Auntie Lucinda, there's a darling. Bye!' And then the door slams and the BMW roars away.

My problem is that they are too busy for me! I've tried whispering till I was blue in the face, I've tried nudging, I've tried dropping hints. *Sometimes* I see a thought actually cloud their eyes, a flicker of conscience, but they quickly shake it off, like someone brushing away an irritating fly or moth. I suppose it won't be long before they send little Benji to a boarding school. I wonder if they will turn up for school plays, or prize-giving, or cricket matches.

I'm worried about Benji. Who knows where these fantasies might lead? And if something isn't done, one day he is going to be very angry and bitter and cynical about his parents. And they are going to be puzzled and hurt, because they believe that they have given him everything that he could possibly need. And they have. Everything except time and affection. I can't get through to them that they are living in a Fool's Paradise. Jesus said, 'Make room for little children, for of such is the Kingdom of Heaven.' I'm afraid Benji's parents don't make much room for him.

Oh dear! The Archangel Gabriel isn't going to be very happy about this report. I suppose that means bang goes my LACG promotion. Ah well, even angels can't win 'em all, but I'll keep trying. I can't grumble really. I've only been at it for about two thousand years, which is just a beginner as far as angels go. Speaking of which this angel has got to. 'Go' I mean. Bye. *(He exits.)*

(Music plays as the lights fade.)

Walliel and the Runaway Girl

WALLIEL *and the* SAR'NT ANGEL *appear in this scene.*

WALLIEL: 'Ello. Angel Walliel 'ere, on a mission from God, as the Blues Brothers might say. Now, my assignment, in a nutshell, is to attempt to get certain children in danger – out of danger. I think I can report, well, a little success. You see, one of the children assigned to me is called Sally. I say 'child' but she's quite a young lady really, eighteen last birthday. The Sar'nt Angel said,

Enter SAR'NT ANGEL.

SAR'NT ANGEL: She is a very worrying case Walliel. Her parents split up, leaving Sally with her mother. Then, her mother found a new boyfriend and, quite simply, moved in with him. Sally was supposed to go and live with her grandmother, but she hasn't done that. She's left home and headed for the bright lights of London. So, my son, you've got to get in there quick! *(He exits.)*

WALLIEL: Before you could say 'Alleluia!' I was at King's Cross Railway Station. Heaven to King's Cross, by special angel flight takes about one millionth of an Earth second. In fact I was in the train before Sally got off. I could see what she was thinking. That's one of the things that angels learn in basic training, 'Thought Interception'.

I can't say that reading her thoughts was easy, because they were a bit of a jumble. In fact she was trying to think something that deep down she didn't believe. She was trying to convince herself that she didn't care, about anything. Her thought argument with herself (it's strange how humans do this, argue with themselves), her thought argument was, that as her mother and father had done exactly what they had wanted, apparently without a thought for anyone else, then there was no reason Sally should care for anyone else, including herself. As the train pulled into the station she was thinking, 'I know what to expect at King's Cross, I've read the Sunday papers, well, I don't care! I'm going to do everything and try everything, and it doesn't matter what happens to me because nothing matters any more.' She was having difficulty with these thoughts because they weren't really her thoughts. There was a little devil hovering around, just over her left shoulder whispering into her ear.

She was carrying her worldly possessions in a very bulky backpack, and as she was struggling down the corridor, I saw what I had been looking for. I was acting on information received from the SIS, the Spiritual Intelligence Service, and they were spot on. There was the young man they had told me about. He wasn't much older than Sally, and he was walking down the train towards her. He couldn't see her because of her backpack, but that didn't matter because he was what we call a 'Receptive', that is someone who is already on the side of the angels.

I was receiving Sally's thoughts loud and clear, she was telling herself a lie. She was saying to herself that she wasn't afraid of anything or anybody, when in fact she was a very frightened young lady. I couldn't hang about, my Guardian Angel's antennae had already detected a motley collection of demons, imps and devils, prowling about the station concourse, waiting to pounce. So I gave this lad the works! Not only did I tell him to help the young lady in front of him with her backpack, but, well, I don't know if I was being rash, or too impulsive, but I dipped into my supply of glory and sprinkled it about liberally. It was in his hair, in his eyes, in his teeth. I hope I didn't overdo it, but when she looked at him she was completely bowled over. And so was he! The trouble with sprinkling glory about in a hurry is that there is no telling where it will go. Quite a bit of it settled on Sally and, well, people on Earth call it 'love at first sight', but in fact, glory in your eyes is the grace of God. Same thing really I suppose.

Sally said, 'Geoff! Geoff Talbot! I haven't seen you since you went away to college! What a coincidence! Where are you going? What are you doing?'

You know, we move Heaven and Earth to arrange meetings like this, but no matter what we do – miracles, anything – humans always say, 'Good heavens! What a coincidence!' I mean, they can't really believe that when people bump into each other, after *years* of *not* bumping into each other, that it just happens by accident! Honestly, people are very naïve.

Well, I don't think I'm going to have much trouble with Sally now. Not for a long time, I hope. Oh dear! Here comes the Sar'nt Angel, and I've just intercepted his thoughts, and he's saying,

The SAR'NT ANGEL *enters. During this next speech, whilst the* SAR'NT ANGEL *is speaking,* WALLIEL *is reciting the same speech, silently, and in synchronisation with the Sar'nt.*

SAR'NT ANGEL: Angel Walliel! What have you been up to? Glory is a very special commodity! And you are showering it around like confetti! I suppose you realise that the engine driver has proposed to the waitress in the buffet car – way ahead of schedule! And who knows what the consequences will be for the people in that compartment! Though I suppose we can be thankful that it has cleared the station of demons, imps and devils. Well, for an hour or two at least. Walliel! Stop reading my thoughts and report at once to the Archangel Gabriel!

WALLIEL and SAR'NT ANGEL: Yes, Sar'nt. Right away Sar'nt.

WALLIEL *exits and the* SAR'NT ANGEL *turns to the audience.*

SAR'NT ANGEL: Two can play at that game you know. I didn't get my sergeant's stripes for nothing.

(Music plays and the lights fade.)

Walliel and the Demon 'Drink'

WALLIEL: I expect you've heard of the expression 'The Demon Drink', but I doubt if you know that there is, in fact, a terrible demon called 'Dyrynk'. That's spelt, D-Y-R-Y-N-K. And he is as nasty a devil as you could hope to meet. Well, I don't suppose you would 'hope' to meet any devil, but you know what I mean. The Demon Dyrynk, is sly and very cunning. Thorough too. He can change good, ordinary people, bring out the worst in them, lead them into lying, cheating and stealing, even killing.

Now, he is not to be confused with drink itself. The produce of grapes, hops and barley fields are all part of God's generous gifts to mankind. They are meant to be enjoyed with gratitude. Our Lord not only enjoyed the fruit of the vine, but, at His last supper, made it holy. Yet evil roams through the world and turns good into bad. The Demon Greed rips out hedgerows and pollutes rivers and seas. The Devil Powerlust misuses chemicals and produces poisons and bombs. No, it would be sacrilege to confuse the Creator's gifts with the misuse of them. And that is what the Demon Dyrynk is devoted to, blinding people to the facts about themselves and God's gifts, pushing people to the point of no return.

No doubt about it, Demon Dyrynk is truly a very nasty piece of work. But recently, he did himself in the eye. I'd been struggling with him, and losing, but, in the end Dyrynk defeated himself.

One of the children that I have been commissioned to keep an eye on is called Samantha. A quiet girl, too quiet, withdrawn, you might say. She can talk, but she doesn't much, mainly on account of her father who has a fierce temper, and her mother who is a secret drinker. Well, she thinks it's secret, but everyone knows, including Samantha and her Dad.

I wondered if it was Dad's furious temper that had

driven her to drink, or her drinking that had made him furious. Anyway, I thought that I'd set to work on Dad first. I thought that if I could nudge him in the direction of controlling his temper then I'd be halfway there, because there were times when he was kind and generous. And at least I could get through to him. You can't really make much headway with someone in an alcoholic stupor. I tried everything. When I saw his temper rising I tried to put happy pictures in his mind, tried to suggest alternative thoughts, reminded him of the early days of their courtship and marriage, but I only made things worse. The more I nudged him in that direction the angrier he seemed to become. It's strange how people who were once very much in love can change their attitude to each other. And so often, the change has started over little things which they never sorted out, little things that have grown out of all proportion.

That wicked devil, the Demon Dyrynk, was having a field day. Every time I put my foot in it, making things worse, I could hear him cackling away, making that horrible noise that devils think is laughter, which is about as far away from a real laugh as Heaven is from Hell. Dyrynk was rolling about, fiendishly delighted and convinced that he had got the upper hand. He was certain that he could do anything he wanted to with this family. He had got them on the slippery slope to misery, and he seemed to be winning. But then, he took a step too far.

Poor Samantha had often seen her mother mindless with drink. One day Dyrynk sidled up to her, and whispered in her ear, with that oily voice of his, 'There's no need to be sad, think of your mother, when she takes her "medicine" she hasn't a care in the world, no worries, no sadness, nothing at all, oblivion. Isn't that a lovely word, oblivion? Wouldn't it be nice to join her, in oblivion?' The Demon led Samantha to one of her mother's secret bottles. It didn't take long for the 'medicine' to work, and soon she fell into a drunken sleep. The bottle, three-quarters full, rolled on to the floor, and the liquid poured out, making a dark, spreading stain on the carpet. The Demon Dyrynk was dancing over her in an ecstasy of evil. I have never felt so low in my entire career as a Guardian Angel. But Dyrynk had overreached himself. It sometimes happens like that. In this case, Samantha's mother found the child and was so horrified that she screamed, a terrible scream, almost as if it wasn't her screaming but something evil escaping from her mouth. Perhaps that's what it was, all the evil that Dyrynk had poured into her, fleeing, terrified at what had been awakened inside Samantha's mother. The deep-seated compassion and love that could no longer be contained.

She didn't cry, not then, but in a kind of rage she ran about the house, teeth clenched in determination, grabbing bottles from all their hiding-places, running into the kitchen or the bathroom or wherever was convenient, bottle after bottle, she poured them all away. When it was done she went back to her child and cradled her in her arms. She wept then.

When Samantha's father came home, her mother was still sitting on the floor with the child in her arms. He just looked at her. I could see that he was deeply moved. Neither of them spoke. It was not necessary. He took the child from her and laid her gently on the settee. Then he took hold of his wife's hands, and very quietly he said, 'Forgive me'. It was very quiet in that room. But I could hear howls disappearing into the ether of the Universe. The words, 'Forgive me' are like a stake through the heart to a demon.

Samantha is a lot happier now. She isn't exactly a chatterbox, but she smiles more. Her parents have a long way to go, but at least they're moving in a new direction, together. And talking of which, I think I'd better move in a new direction too. Bye. *(He exits.)*

(Music plays as the lights fade.)

Walliel and the Little Perisher

WALLIEL: One of my special children is called Roger. Now the problem with Roger is that he steals things. But he doesn't steal things for himself. At first he started shoplifting to give things to boys at school, mainly because he wanted them to accept him as a friend. Sadly, it didn't work. Well, it did for about five minutes, but quite soon they went off and they made it very clear that Roger was not wanted. He's a strange boy, Roger. It's as if he knows that he's not wanted and somehow he communicates this feeling to other people.

It didn't take long for me to discover why he was not wanted at home. His mother was living with a man who was not Roger's father and he didn't want him, and his mother didn't seem to care for him too much either. 'Little perisher' she called him. 'I hope that little perisher gives us some peace tonight. God knows what he's doing up in that room of his, little perisher.' Of course God knew what the little perisher was doing in his room. He was sorting out his pickings from the shops, deciding whose friendship might be won for five minutes in the school playground.

His mother always fed and clothed the little perisher. She obviously believed that if she did this she had done her duty and was as good a mother as any other mother. Her conscience was clear, and nothing else was required of her.

I often wonder how people think they will justify their lives before God. Did Roger's mother really believe that she could stand face to face with the God of Love and say 'Well, I did my duty. I fed and clothed him, he never went in need of anything.' Did she really believe that her little perisher had no other needs?

I don't know how Roger met up with with Mrs

Springer, but somehow he did. Perhaps he met her at the cinema where she works. The man who lives with Roger's mother often gave him some money to go to the pictures. It wasn't so much a gesture of kindness as a method of getting Roger out of the house for a few hours. However they met, they met. She would chat with him as they walked along, either to or from the cinema, because Roger had made a point of walking down the street at the same time as Mrs Springer. And then he started to steal for her. At first it was just a handkerchief which he said was an unwanted Christmas present of his mother's. But when he gave her an expensive silk scarf she knew that something was wrong. At first she didn't know what to do. She didn't want to get the boy into trouble, but she knew unless Roger's stealing was stopped, eventually he would be caught, and who knew what the consequences of that might be.

She had become quite fond of Roger and his funny conversations about things that were, to her, inconsequential, but to him were of very great importance; about football teams and sportsmen she had never heard of. She knew where Roger lived. She had seen him go into the little terraced house in Walker Street. She wondered if she should speak to his mother and had nearly got as far as knocking on the door. But as she had approached the house a youngish woman was leaving. Her clothes were very, well, what Mrs Springer's mother used to call 'blousey', too loud and far too tight. A man was waiting for her on the steps. He looked hardfaced and was clearly impatient.

The young woman had turned in the doorway and shouted to someone inside, 'Now don't you forget, you little perisher! You be in bed before ten o'clock, if you don't want to see the back of 'Arry's hand! All right?' And from inside the house Mrs Springer had heard Roger's voice shouting, 'All right!'

Mrs Springer had known then that she couldn't talk to Roger's mother about stealing. It was later, when she was ironing that she had decided what she would do.

The next day, as Mrs Springer and Roger began their regular walk from the cinema, she took hold of his arm and looked at him very seriously. 'Roger,' she said. 'Do you think you would be clever enough to return the handkerchief and the scarf to where you got them from, without anyone knowing?' Roger, who was rather proud of his ability to move things around without people seeing, blurted out, 'Course! Easy!' And then he noticed how serious Mrs Springer's face was and he suddenly realised the significance of what she was saying. He began to blush.

Now, Mrs Springer's Guardian Angel is called Rachael, and she had clearly kept in close touch with Mrs Springer over the years, and had looked after her spiritual health very well indeed, though it must have been a help that Mrs Springer was a 'Receptive'. You know, that's what we Guardian Angels call people who are already on our side in the battle.

'You don't have to give me things, you know,' she said to Roger. 'I like you just as you are. I had a son once, just like you, but he died.' Then Angel Rachael must have dropped exactly the right words into Mrs Springer's ears, because suddenly she said, 'I've got an idea! I have no family now, so perhaps I could be a kind of Auntie to you. You could call me Auntie Mary. Would you like that?' For the first time that Mrs Springer could remember his serious little face broke into a really beautiful smile. Of course it was all down to Angel Rachael, releasing some of her supply of glory at exactly the right moment. I must say her timing was perfect. You have probably guessed by now, that in Heaven 'glory' is one of the many angelic words for love. That's our secret. Love is our armour, our weapon and our wings. And talking of wings, I must fly. Bye! *(He exits.)*

(Music plays as the lights fade.)

The Eye of My Mind

In the eye of my mind
there's a love song.
In the eye of my mind
I'm still young.
In the eye of my mind
there's a love song
that's waiting some day
to be sung.

Hop-scotch and marbles,
and grown-ups are kind,
lullabies and laughter
dance in my mind.
Lollipops and birthdays
and games that we play,
pictures of childhood
now fading away;

where is the world
that was offered to me,
the caring, the sharing,
the life that was free?
Where are the people
who said it was true
that if you loved the world
then the world would love you?

Wide-eyed and truthful,
that's my young man,
eagerly willing
to give all he can;
memories of promises
of love amongst men,
a world of no wars
and no fighting again;

a world of no hunger,
a world that is one,
a world holding hands
while the laughter goes on;
where are the people
who said it was true
that if you loved the world
then the world would love you?

Are children so simple
or grown-ups so bad?
Does the idea of loving
belong to the mad?
Is the road to the land
of all sweetness and honey
guarded with missiles
and cobbled with money?

Are justice and freedom
mere figures of fun?
Is reality only
the smoke from a gun?
Is goodness just weakness?
Is hope merely pain?
For if that is wisdom,
who wants to be sane?

THE EYE OF MY MIND

In the eye of my mind
there's a love song.
In the eye of my mind
I'm still young.
In the eye of my mind
there's a love song
that's waiting some day
to be sung.

Eh Brian!

This is a solo speech. The speaker is the teenage brother of Brian, also a teenager. The speech is addressed initially and finally to Brian. The middle verses are addressed directly to the audience. The 'Gerroffs' refer to light punches received from Brian, and one from 'Dad'. Lights fade up, preferably a single pool of light, isolating the speaker.

BRIAN'S BROTHER: Eh Brian!
You growing a tash
or drinking cocoa?

. . . Gerroff! It was only a joke!

No, it looks all right.
A judicious application
of Barbara's eyebrow pencil
might improve it though,
Mary Quant, Number Four.

. . . Gerroff! It was only a joke!

He shouldn't have done that,
slammed the door.
He'll wake the old man,
and he's got a big day tomorrow,
signing on.

. . . Eh Dad! Gerroff! It was only a
joke!

It's the real thing though,
must be,
'cos I've never seen the mandarin
shirt
And the Bowie trousers,
on a Tuesday.

And, he's shaving twice a day,
because,
in the magnified side of Dad's
mirror
he *thought* he saw a hair,
and he's trying to encourage the
growth.

Yeah, he's got it bad.
He's spending
as if the Social Security
was made of money.
To my certain knowledge,
with reckless abandon,
he's bought two Oral B
toothbrushes
this month.
If that's not love,
what is?

Hello Brian.
That was quick
is she sick, or washing her hair?

. . . AAEH!! Gerroff!! It was only a
joke!

A slight pause as BRIAN'S BROTHER *looks closely at Brian.*

Eh, Brian,
you crying?

(The light slowly fades.)

The Contender

The Contender *is a one-sided telephone conversation. Props required: Chair, Table and Telephone.*

The speech was written with a New York, Brooklyn, accent in mind, but it could be adapted to whatever US accent the actor is most familiar with.

Suggestion: Some wild Israeli folk dance music. Lights fade up to spotlight man sitting alongside the table. He is dialling a number.

HARRY: *(After waiting to be connected.)* Hey Ben! How ya keeping? It's a long time. How's the family? That's great! Give Edna a big hug from me huh? Hey Ben, put me through to the man, will ya? Wadda ya mean, what man? The King, Saul, ya know, the guy with a crown and a kingsized headache about Public Enemy Number One . . . Public Enemy Number One! A punk called Goliath . . . *Go-li-ath*! He's a heavy for the Philistine mob . . . Uh-huh. Hey kid, you got it. Now can I speak with Saul, you remember him, King of the Israelites? . . . He's in with who? . . . The musicians and the dancing girls, and he doesn't want to be distoibed. Hey that's beautiful, but I've got music that's gonna blow his royal mind. Like I've found a hit man to take out Goliath. So stop playing the momma-hen and put me through to the man, Ben . . . What's that? Well Ben, I got news for ya, you're gonna be in trouble whither way, because if you don't put me through I'm gonna see to it, poissonally, that ya head rolls . . . Uh-huh? . . . Huh, well, I love you too Ben.

Hello, it's Harry . . . Yeah . . . Saul, remember you told me, you were ready to put out a contract on a gorilla called Goliath? . . . Well I've got a mechanic who's a hit man like no other guy you ever heard of . . . No, I didn't bring him in, he volunteered, er, like, a voice in his head said, er, he gotta do this thing . . . What is his record? Well, he's not trained in *exactly* this kind of work, but . . . What does he do? Well, er, Saul you're gonna laugh, but, er, huh, right now he looks after his Daddy's sheep . . . Saul, would I joke about a thing like this? Hey, what can I tell ya? When it comes to homicide, this kid is dynamite . . . What does he use? . . . No, he's not a knife man . . . No, no, er not artillery. Hey, listen Saul, he slings rocks . . . No, not boulders, rocks, little rocks, like pebbles . . . Well, no, he's not a very big guy. He weighs in at about a hundred and twenty-six pounds . . . Sure, I know Goliath is about three times bigger, and the kid knows that. But Saul, this kid can KO a rattlesnake at a hundred yards. He even wasted a lion that was mauling his Daddy's sheep. I figure that we ain't got anybody who's gonna match Goliath pound for pound, but this kid will take him . . . Saul, I know there's a lot hanging in on this fight, but I checked him out, he's fast and he's deadly. The thing is you don't believe it till ya see it. He's such a good-looking kid, big, innocent eyes, a curly mop. I tell ya, Goliath will underestimate the kid. He might even laugh. If he does, it'll be the last thing he does on earth. Ya know the old proverb, pride comes before a fall? Believe me, Goliath is gonna fall . . . Chief, I'm willing to stake my shield on the kid. Hey, you better remember this kid's name, because he's going places. He's called David . . . Saul, you will not regret this. OK I'll bring him round for the fight, Tuesday. Hey Saul? Do me a favour? Save me a ringside will ya? 'Cos this David versus Goliath is one fight I don't want to miss . . . What's that? . . . Front row? . . . Next to you? . . . Hey Saul, who loves ya baby?

(Music: lights fade.)

Abraham and Sarah

This script was first broadcast on BBC Radio 2 in the style of the North Country radio comedian, Rob Wilton. His famous catch phrase with which he began his broadcasts was, 'The day war broke out . . .'

It is a tribute to him that he has had so many imitators, and that his catch phrases are still well known.

In this sketch, the Rob Wilton character plays the part of the Old Testament patriarch, Abraham. The form is based on one of his rhyming monologues.

ABRAHAM: The day my wife found out
she was going to have a baby,
three very funny fellers
called at our tent.

They said, 'Are you Abe?'
I said, 'Aye.'
'From where?'
I said, 'Ur.'
They said, 'Where?'
I said, 'Ur, in the Chaldees,
ask anyone, they'll tell yer.'

They said, 'If he's Abe, from Ur,
there's a babe for her,'
and she laughed,
'cos it was daft,
'er being eighty last year.
Well, yer would, wouldn't yer?

Then the Lord came along
and said it was wrong,
to laugh at the news that He'd sent.
He said, 'If you don't believe
that you can conceive,
I think it's time that I went.'

She said, 'Laugh? D'yer mean me?'
He said, 'Aye, I mean thee.'
She said, 'No.'
He said, 'Oh?
Then tell me my dear,
just how did I hear
that snort – through the vent,
in the tent?'

Well, there was nowt she could do,
she knew it was true,
and there's nowt yer can hide,
from Him.

He said, 'Abraham,
you'll be pushing a pram
before another year's through.'
I said, 'Who?'
He said, 'You.'
'Is that right?'
He said, 'True!'
Well, there's nowt He doesn't know!

I said to the wife,
'Now Sarah, yer must,
when it comes to the Lord,
learn how to trust,
'cos He never breaks His promise,
yer know.'

So, if there's one thing we've learned,
the wife, and me,

it's, wherever we go,
He'll be.
Before us, behind us,
over and under,
and all we can do
is sit and wonder.

Well,
we've walked many a mile
but it still makes me smile
when the little un's takin' a bath,
'cos the Lord's little game
is in Isaac's name,
it means, don't you know,
'He will laugh!'

Herod and the Child

HEROD THE GREAT: *At this stage of his life Herod was suffering from a disease which eventually drove him insane. His success was due to treachery, intrigue and considerable personal ability in several fields.*

He was an outstanding soldier and battle commander. In those areas of combat in which he was the sole commander, he never lost a battle.

He was an extremely astute politician and a ruthless king with more than a touch of megalomania. N.B. Not a Jew but an Idomite.

ELI BAR SIMON: *A high-ranking soldier who has fought many campaigns with* HEROD. *He is a veteran of many battles. He is a Jew and currently responsible for* HEROD'S *personal safety.*

HEROD *is standing looking at the sky.*
Offstage we can hear the stamp of soldiers' feet, and voices shouting 'Sir!'
ELI BAR SIMON *is acknowledging their salute as he enters.*

ELI: Sir.

HEROD: Eli, look. *(He points to the sky.)*
There they are.
What do you think?

ELI: They are – extraordinary, Sir.

HEROD: Yes, but what do you think?
You have ears in every seditious gathering,
what is being said?

ELI: About the stars?

HEROD: Don't play the fool, Eli.
What is being said?

ELI: Nothing about stars, Sir.
Apart from the astronomers,
no one has mentioned them.
There are complaints about the census,
people suspect, in the end,
it will mean more taxes.
Which of course it will.
They complain about the crowds,
people and animals block every street.
Innkeepers and thieves make fortunes,
but no one says anything about stars.

It's almost as if they hadn't noticed them,
or cannot even see them perhaps?
With so many light-fingered rogues about
people keep their eyes on their money.
In the market, they say,
'Sneeze, and lose your purse.'

HEROD: Seven months!
For at least seven months
they have been there,
the brightest lights in the evening sky
and nobody has noticed?

ELI: Apparently not, Sir.
Apart from the visiting astronomers,
and your own night-sky watchers.

HEROD: My night-sky watchers, as you call them,
my scholars, my advisors,
advise me of nothing!

Look at them, Eli.
Sword in hand

you have waited for more dawns
than most men.
Have you ever seen such a sky?

ELI: No, Sir.
No sky, and certainly no star
as bright as that.

HEROD: Is it one star, or two?
So conjoined that, almost,
they compete for precedence
with the moon.
And those imbeciles say
it implies nothing?

(He mimics his advisors.)

'Nothing to trouble your Majesty's council.'

Filthy schemers! And stupid!
Do they think I don't know
that the heavens leap
in anticipation
of calamitous events?
Did they think I was deaf
when Sutonius spoke of stars
being jettisoned from their course
even as Caesar staggered
in the midst of his murderers?

Soothsayers wailed
about celestial signs
days before Brutus wiped the blood
from his blade.
Is it possible
that I would not perceive
the connection
between Caesar's star and mine,
when I was established procurator
by the same Caesar?

Do they think the Gods
have not cast me in the same play?
Or that Herod is not involved
in the intrigues of Olympus?

Eli – what are they saying?

ELI: Hyrcanus has advised his people
to show no favour to the Romans
beyond what is required by law.
But he also advises them
to be scrupulous
in all their dealings,
buying, selling, paying taxes.
He fears that the military
are looking for an excuse
to suppress Zealots.

HEROD: To show no favour?
To be scrupulous?
Oh that is rich!
Is he now pretending
to righteousness?

I first came to power
through the costly favour
of Mark Antony.
To secure this crown,
in the gift of Caesar Augustus,
I filled Mark Antony's coffers
to the brim.
But that double-dealing Hasmonean
in Jerusalem, Hyrcanus,
purchased the robes of a High Priest
with as much blood and money
as I did my crown.
And now the hypocrite dares to speak
of scruples?

He, of all people, knows
it is not by scruples that we survive!

He's up to something.

Have you noticed how obsequious
my council have been?
Full of sycophantic, flowery nonsense
but saying nothing?

ELI: They're frightened.

HEROD: They're always frightened,
and with good reason.
But you are not afraid of me, Eli,
you never have been.
I doubt if you fear man, god or devil.

ELI: I fear God.

HEROD: Yes, but not as they do.
You are not a religious man,
not what I call religious.
But you are a Jew, and therefore acceptable.
Whereas they say of me,
'Herod is not a Jew, he's an Idomite!
A Barbarian! A usurper of power!
And worse, a friend of Rome.'

(Laughs.)

They do not know me, do they, Eli?
Herod's only friend is Herod,
and perhaps you, Eli Bar Simon, perhaps
you?

(ELI smiles, a very small smile.)

HEROD: And you know, Eli,
that I have tried to play the friend,
proffered the olive branch.
Marrying the Hasmonean girl
was not entirely political expedience
Mariamne was a very beautiful woman,

hardly a woman, a child.
And she bore me sons.

(He thinks about it.)

Yet even while my bed
was still warm with her passion
she and her high-born Hasmonean family
plotted my death.
Scruples?
My scruples wrapped themselves about her
  neck
and perished with her,
and her scrupulous brother,
and especially her conniving mother!

Have you ever wanted to kill me, Eli?

ELI: *(After a brief reflection.)* Yes.

HEROD: *(Looks sharply at* ELI, *and then laughs.)*

Oh! Eli Bar Simon!
Only you could say that to my face.
And why have you *not* killed me?

ELI: Because more than once, in battle,
you have saved my life.
And because whatever they say about you
I know that you have supplied the people
with food in famine,
paid ransoms, rebuilt the temple,
honoured Jerusalem with a palace,
and extended the city.
You have humoured the Romans
with towns like Caesarea,
fought battles, and for nearly forty years,
you have kept the peace in this cauldron.
You did not inherit the title 'Great',
you earned it.
And that, Sir, is not sycophancy but fact.

In a word, Sir,
killing you would not help my people.

HEROD: Then God help me if it ever would.
Though, if you were to kill me,
you are not the man to plot and scheme, are you?
Nor would you stab me in the back.
You would meet me face to face, dagger drawn.
Yes, I'd prefer that.

Oh, I did like that bit, er,
about the title.
What did you say?
I did not inherit the title 'Great'
I earned it. Very good!
But the great, as you know, Eli,
are surrounded always
by treachery and conspiracy.
As I have been
since before my beard sprouted.
You at least understand
why I cannot have scruples.

(He moves to a seat and sits.)

Only the poor can afford scruples.

(He laughs.)

That's good don't you think?
– only the poor can afford scruples –
You ought to write it down, Eli,
there's nothing historians like better
than a royal aphorism.
And then my sons can quote me
to my grandsons.

(HEROD falls silent. ELI watches him like a doctor with a patient. He is very familiar with Herod's manic moods.)

HEROD: *(He is very sombre.)* Eli, Eli,

Who poisoned their minds?

Alexander and Aristobulus were the best of my sons.
I sent them to Rome, to learn statecraft.
They were proud of me.
We used to play games together.
Aristobulus was such a fool, full of laughter.
We used to weep with laughing.
He could imitate people, you know,
the way they spoke, the way they moved.
The members of the council, and their wives.
Once, they dressed up, and played a love scene,
Alexander as Mark Antony
and Aristobulus as Cleopatra.
Oh they were such . . . such . . .

Who filled their ears
with such murderous mischief? Who? Eli, who?

I had to do it!
I had to act swiftly!
They raised a force of three hundred men!

ELI: You suppressed a rebellion, Sir.

HEROD: I killed my own sons!

ELI: They did not intend to spare you.
They would not have sent you into exile, Sir,
they intended to take your crown and your life.

HEROD: They could hardly have done one without the other.
Hyrcanus talked of exile,
exile for the ringleaders.

Well they are exiled now, in Hell!
Where sedition and treachery can roam at will
and eternally plot the downfall of Satan
himself
with as much success as they plotted mine!

Why? Eli Bar Simon, why?
Why does treachery crawl
through every crack and crevice
in this kingdom?

The dust has hardly settled
on the graves of my sons
and I am presented
with more omens and signs
of yet another pretender to my throne!

When those three travellers
with all the confidence of their rank
came bustling in here
with talk of stars, and heavenly bodies,

(Mimics old man.)

'Which predict the coming of a king.'
I could have slit their throats
even as they babbled!

By their calculations
the vicinity of Bethlehem
is to be the scene of this momentous event.
Bethlehem? Bethlehem?
It's a dung heap!

They've been gone too long.
I should have bribed them.

Did you say they came from Babylon?

ELI: Yes, Sir.

HEROD: Babylon, Babylon.
There's a wild country,

full of barbarous beliefs.
Now what's . . .
what's the cult that thrives there?

ELI: The cult of Zoroaster.

HEROD: And what do they believe?

ELI: They have a fantastic belief
that a 'Sanshyant', a saviour of the people,
will be born – of a virgin.

HEROD: A virgin?

ELI: That's what they believe.

HEROD: But why have the Gods misdirected him
to Bethlehem?
It's a Babylonian cult,
it would have been better for him
to have been born in Babylon.

ELI: Sir, even if this incredible idea was true,
your kingdom cannot, surely, be threatened
by a child?

(HEROD *roars, and in a fit of rage grabs hold of* ELI.)

HEROD: My kingdom was threatened by my own children!
My own flesh and blood!
Do you think I'm going to take a chance
on some other brat?

(He pushes Eli to one side.)

A child. A child.

(He is now talking to himself.)

That's it. Find the child.
But a child amongst how many.

A hundred? – A thousand? – More?
No matter, I'll find him.
I must.

(He sees ELI *and smiles, but continues to talk to himself.)*

They call me an Idomite barbarian, hm?
Well, give a dog a bad name.
I could teach them a lesson, in barbarity.
A lesson that would not be forgotten,
not in my lifetime.
Still, if I intend to die in my bed . . .

(He continues to muse to himself, in silence, before eventually reaching a decision.)

Eli! Inform the Guard Commander
that I have a task for him
. . . in Bethlehem.

Jesus Candles

This is a song for children, of all ages!

CHORUS

Jesus candles, burning bright,
Gold and yellow, blue and white,
Jesus candles, bring His light,
His love and His laughter
To the dark of the night.

VERSE 1

Oh you can't sweep the dark with a broom
And a frown will not chase it away;
But a smile lifts the gloom
And love lights a room
And prayer turns the night into day.
So I'll light a candle for Jesus my Lord,
A flame that will never depart,
A glow that will show that He is adored
And my Lord is the light of my heart.

CHORUS: Jesus candles, burning bright . . .

VERSE 2

There are lanterns we light with a prayer
That will guide us in age and in youth;
If with Jesus we share
Our joy and our care,
Oh we'll find the way and the truth.

So I'll light a candle for Jesus my guide,
For Jesus my shepherd and friend,
For He would like me to walk by His side
And abide in His light without end.

CHORUS: Jesus candles, burning bright . . .

VERSE 3

As the light of the world Jesus came,
Bringing gifts from His Father above;
Now the weak and the lame
Sing praise to His name
And rejoice in the light of His love.
So I'll light a candle for love that never dies,
To kindle His loving in me
And pray for the day when the light of His eyes
Will surprise with His love eternally.

CHORUS: Jesus candles, burning bright . . .

Jesus Candles

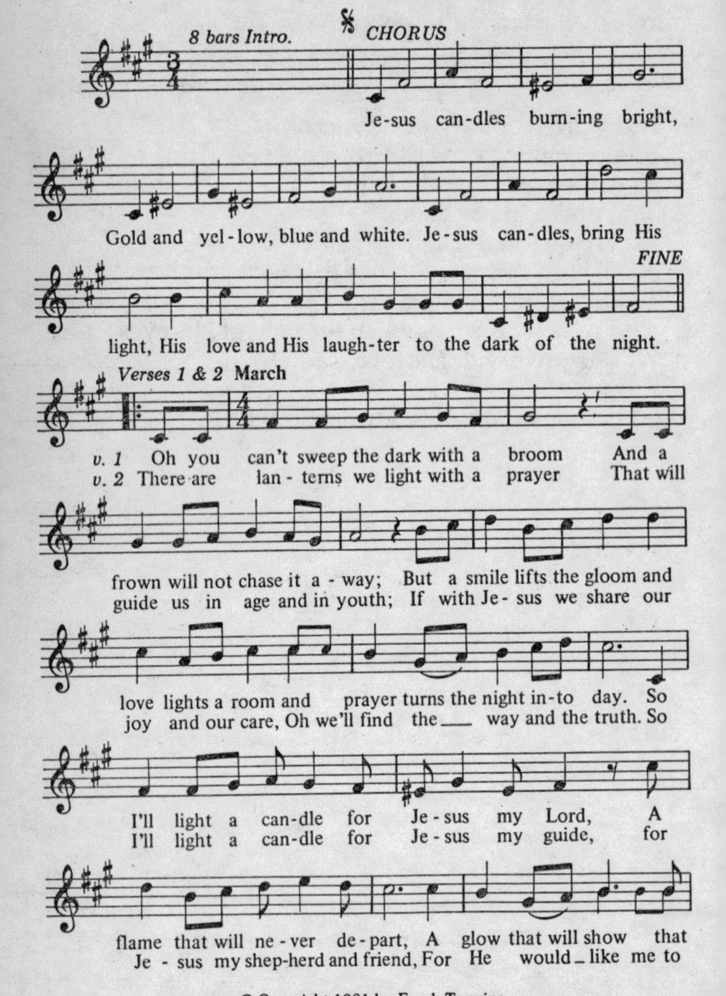

JESUS CANDLES

The Battle of Jericho

This is a telephone conversation between one of Joshua's senior army officers and the chief armourer of Joshua's army. It takes place a week before the battle.

It was written with the voice of the American actor, Bob Newhart, in mind.

Spotlighted area, lights fade up to reveal actor holding a telephone receiver to his ear.

Hello! Hello, Ben, it's er, it's, it's good to speak with you, Ben. Huh? . . . Oh fine, fine . . . yeah . . . she's fine too . . . Er, Ben, d'ye know next week's battle? At Jericho . . . Ssh! Not too loud, you never know who's . . . What? The enemy is not on the phone? Er, er, how, how do you know that? . . . Be-be-because it hasn't been invented yet . . .

Well, Ben, about the battle of er, Jericho, er, well, d-d-do you know the three thousand ladders that you had made, to scale the walls? . . . Yeah, well, gee, I don't know how to tell you this Ben, but er, we ain't gonna need them . . . No, they're beautiful, they're beautiful ladders, Ben, it's just that they're out. And the same goes for the battering rams, and the rock-slinging catapults. They're all out . . . Well, don't take it out on me, Ben, I'm not the General, I just pick up the cheque, ye know? . . . What? . . . What, what are they going to use instead? Well, you know Joshua, he's a kind of individual feller. He, he's going to use, er, priests . . . What? . . . I said priests . . . What do you mean, 'What kind of priests?' The holy kind, the praying kind, you know, come Saturday they wish you Shabbat Shalom . . . that's right, that kind of priest . . . What? . . . Oh, how many priests? Uh, seven . . . No, not seven thousand. Just seven, you know, six and one . . . Do they get issued with equipment? Oh yeah, a very special kind of equipment, er . . . horns. Rams' horns . . . what do you mean you don't stock rams' horns? Well, you'll just have to go out and get some, Ben. Hey, there's a place on the corner of fifth and twelfth, they do a beautiful line in rams' horns.

. . . What? What's that? What are they going to do with them? . . . Ha! Ha! That's very funny. They're going to put them on their heads and ram the gates . . . er, no Ben, they're not going to do that. No, well, er . . . Hey, will you listen, Ben, just listen and I'll tell you what we're gonna do. See, er, everybody gets to go to Jericho, right? Everybody. And for six days we circle the city, keeping schtum, er, quiet, silent, not a word, see? And then, on the seventh day everybody gets to shout like crazy, and the priests blow their horns, and then, and then, er, you gotta believe me Ben, but Joshua says, er, Joshua says, the walls are going to fall down. Ha-ha!

. . . Hello? Ben? Are you still there? Hey, Ben, you know I sometimes think that you haven't got what it takes for this job . . . Hm? Well, I mean like faith, Ben, like faith. Cos with a battle plan like this, that you gotta have!!!

(Lights fade to blackout.)

PRISONS

The four prison sketches can be performed separately or as a sequence, with one actor or four. In a production for television the director also cast actors in the non-speaking roles of the occupants of the various cells. Despite the fact that they do not speak, a lot of fun can be made from portraying the characters they represent. The prison cells can be realistic, suggested, or not represented at all. Both cells and occupants are described within the text. The visitors being shown around are the audience.

Sound effects for all sketches are the same. As the lights are coming up there should be atmosphere created by the sounds of keys rattling, locks being turned, heavy doors creaking or hinges squealing. Each sketch should end with a blackout and a loud echoey slam of a prison door.

Pride Prison is presented by a very 'plummy' SUPERCILIOUS CHARACTER.

Time Prison is presented by a NERVOUS, 'White Rabbit' CHARACTER.

Lethargy Lodge is presented by the COCKNEY WARDER, a 'Cheeky Chappy'.

Mount Mammon Money Prison is presented by a very smooth AMERICAN.

Pride Prison

SUPERCILIOUS CHARACTER: Ah! . . . visitors. I won't welcome you, because of course you have all been here before. As prisoners. Though I doubt if you will have done quite as much time as I have. I have been in various prisons throughout my life, off and on, in and out. But I know this place, Pride Prison, better than most.

You know the rules, so while you are here you ought to be vile enough to observe them strictly. Fail to observe the rules of Pride Prison and I warn you, you will suffer the indignity of learning such things as charity, cheek turning and other debasing practices.

Let us remind ourselves of the strictures of Pride Prison. Here, in Pride, naturally one is prevented from asking for favours, even when one is entitled to them. A lapse from this rule could put one in the invidious position of having to accept kindnesses. Pride also does not allow friendships between people who do not have the same status. In Pride Prison, if you are working class, then we insist that your only real friends come from the same class, and this applies to all classes throughout Pride Prison.

In Pride Prison it is forbidden to mend broken friendships – to reconstruct broken friendships requires a certain amount of . . . bending . . . on both sides – a loathsome practice. Pride expressly forbids it. Not that everything is negative here. There are things to look forward to. For instance, in Pride Prison you are awarded good conduct marks, for such things as vanity, pomposity and arrogance. Naturally we are all vain, though in different ways. There's physical vanity, and intellectual vanity. Physical vanity needs no explanation. Intellectual vanity, however, can be more subtle. For example, there are a few here who boast that they are spiritually superior to other men . . . 'holier than thou', would be putting it mildly. They contest the holiness of God in comparison with their own piety. There are not many in that group. Most of us here have already vanquished God. After all, He is nothing but a childish idea in the minds of those to whom we are superior.

I notice that some of you want to go . . . well that's not surprising. Only the very best stay in Pride Prison. I won't ask you if you have enjoyed your visit. You wouldn't admit it. After all, even you have your Pride. Good day.

Time Prison

As lights fade up an actor hurries on to the stage. He is about to speak to the audience when he is stopped by the ringing of a bell. He appears nervous and twitchy, constantly checking the time on one of his many watches. (This could be quite pantomimic.) He speaks very quickly.

NERVOUS CHARACTER: Hello. Oh dear, oh, I'm afraid, I'm afraid I can't spare you very much time – you see this is Time Prison, and that's the trouble here. We haven't got it, I mean there isn't any, time that is. It's very difficult to serve time when it keeps running out on you. Well I'd better try and fit you in or you'll only keep coming back and that would be a waste of . . . oh, too dreadful to contemplate. And what am I doing, procrastinating, and that is the thief of . . .

Well, er, Time is an open pris . . . good heavens – is that the time? Look, I really must be, em, I think the best thing is to show you a few of the inmates, very quickly I'm afraid, you see there's not a lot of t . . . It's amazing how much time you can waste telling people that you haven't . . . oooh! (*Consults yet another watch.*) The tempus is absolutely . . . fugitting! Let me pick a few examples.

Now everyone here has been convicted of not having time. Yes . . . for instance, Prisoner 2.45, Blenkinsop A., The Reverend, has been convicted of not having time – for his family. He's spent years in his study, visiting parishioners, attending meetings, night and day, and working every weekend . . . never had time for his wife, never had time to play with his children . . . too busy doing good works. A common case that amongst the clergy.

And here is Prisoner 2.15, Carruthers B. This is a man who could have got on in the world if only he'd had time to train for something. He has frequently been offered the opportunity of further education, career courses, management training, night school – but unfortunately, he never had the time to join any of those courses, which is why he was assistant to the under clerks assistant for forty-three years.

Oh, now if you just look into that cell there you can see Prisoner 4.40, Beacon C. You will deduce from all the reference books that Mr Beacon is a very well-informed man. He knows about all the world's trouble spots, he can tell you the diet of the average Indian pauper, quote the exact number of refugees on the road to Timbuktu, knows how many H-bombs there are in America and Russia, and the precise year the world's oil supply will run out, and as you can imagine, he's a very worried man. He can frequently be heard saying that someone ought to do something about it. Unfortunately he can't do anything himself. No time you see – all those newspapers to keep up with . . .

Oh yes, there's Prisoner 3.27, Goodenough H. Basically he's a very religious man. Well at least he would have been except that he found that he never had much time to think about things like God. After all he had his career to think about. Weekends? Sunday? Well, there again you know what Sunday's like. There's the car to wash, the back room to paint, the garden. I mean there isn't time to do everything, is there?

Now Prisoner 10.30, Jones P. Oh – I'm afraid he isn't with us any more, poor chap, came to the end of his time you see. *(Alarm bell rings.)* Oh . . . good heavens . . . so have I. Bye!

Lethargy Lodge

COCKNEY WARDER: Good morning. This is Lethargy Lodge Open Prison for prisoners convicted of inertia. It's a very comfortable prison here; prisoners can do what they like all day long. The trouble is none of them actually do anything – in fact, doing nothing is their principal occupation. I mean, they've got things that they would like to do, but they never actually get round to doing them. Some prisoners *feel* very strongly on all sorts of issues, but they never do anything about them. I mean, look at Lethargic Larry watching the television – in fact, he's always watching television. Larry will watch anything: children's programmes, current affairs, plays, documentaries – he even spends a couple of hours each day watching the test card. The programme he's watching at the moment, he don't like it. I mean, I can tell that – I can tell he don't like it because he's muttering to himself. See that? Look! Mutter, mutter, mutter, mutter! You see? But he won't do nothing. I mean he could protest to the TV company; he could write a complaining letter to the press; he could contact his MP, or he could, if he made the effort, change the station, or, dare I suggest it, he could even switch off. But he wouldn't do that. No, no, he wouldn't do that, because without telly he'd have to *do* something – like read a book, or go for a walk, or take up stamp collecting, join an amateur operatic society, or stand for parliament. So he just sits there muttering. There he goes, look – mutter, mutter, mutter.

Now the fellow next door, he's just as bad – Stevie Stagnant. The cell he's living in used to be a very nice cell, with a lovely view out the window, lovely cell it was. But the prison planners came along and they decided it would be better to move his bed to the other wall, which they did, only now he can't see out the window. But he didn't say nothing. Then they decide to put the prison motor pump and generator in the corner of his cell, seeing as he didn't complain about the bed being moved. It makes a terrible row when it is switched on, that generator, and the smoke – well, it makes 'im cough. You and I would have cut up nasty about that, but Stevie Stagnant, he don't do nothing about it. I mean, he could have tried to stop them moving his bed, or he could have argued the toss about the generator, but no, he just sits there looking sad – and coughing.

Over there sits Ernie Idle. 'E's got a comfortable pad; yer see 'e's a trusty: he gets two of everyfing – extra blankets, extra 'elpings of pudding. Now 'e knows it ain't right, getting more than anybody else. I mean, 'e could always share his fings. But does he? Nah! He just eats his extra helpings and feels terribly guilty about it. Terribly guilty.

Can you see that bell up there? That's the exit bell. Well now, all of them could leave at any time they want. All they have to do is to go and ring that bell and – well, they don't do that because, to tell the truth, they don't like to make a fuss. Tarra then!

Mount Mammon Money Prison

AMERICAN VOICE: Hi there! Welcome to Mount Mammon Money Prison, the jail with a difference. You see, all the inmates of Mount Mammon Money Prison enter voluntarily – the only condition is that you have to want more than you've got. In fact the people in here not only want more than they've got, but they have devoted their whole lives to getting it. For example, the man in this cell here. This is Harim H. P. Purchase – better known to his friends as Never-Never Sam. Now Never-Never Sam's cell is really very beautiful. He has deep pile carpet on the floor, leather Chesterfield furniture, a hi-fi stereo, television-cum-cocktail cabinet, all fully automatic, as seen on television. And there's Never-Never Sam sitting at his desk. He's the guy with the green eyeshade, biting the fingernails of one hand whilst writing out cheques with the other. Now he doesn't look very happy at the moment, but he says when he gets through paying for all this, life is going to be just great.

In the next cell is Big G; Mr G. G. L. Someday – that stands for, 'Gotta Get the Loot Someday'. Mr Someday's cell is very bare. There is absolutely nothing in his cell except the pile of newspapers and magazines which tell Mr Someday how to make a fortune by gambling. Now he hasn't got it all worked out just yet; but he's working on the perfect roulette system, added to which he has just joined a syndicate that practically ensures him a big win on the British Football Pools. So how can he lose – yet?

The cell next door belongs to Ticker-Tape Tom. Now Ticker-Tape Tom really has made it big. He's a very wealthy man. His cell is almost entirely taken up by a ticker-tape machine, and that's Ticker-Tape Tom bending over the machine watching the ticker-tape come through. He watches that machine all day long. You see, the trouble is if you have got lots of stocks, shares and bonds, why you've just gotta keep your eye on that ticker-tape machine, 'cos man, the bottom could drop out of the market any day; so Ticker-Tape Tom keeps his eye glued to that ticker-tape machine.

Like I said, all the inmates of Mount Mammon Money Prison enter voluntarily. You can come and go just as you please. There's the exit door down there, and you can leave any time you like. There's a condition though. It's printed on that notice just over the exit door. I don't know if you can read it from where you are, but it says – (*little laugh*) – oh yes, 'You can't take it with you when you go.'